SPIRIT
OF THE HARVEST

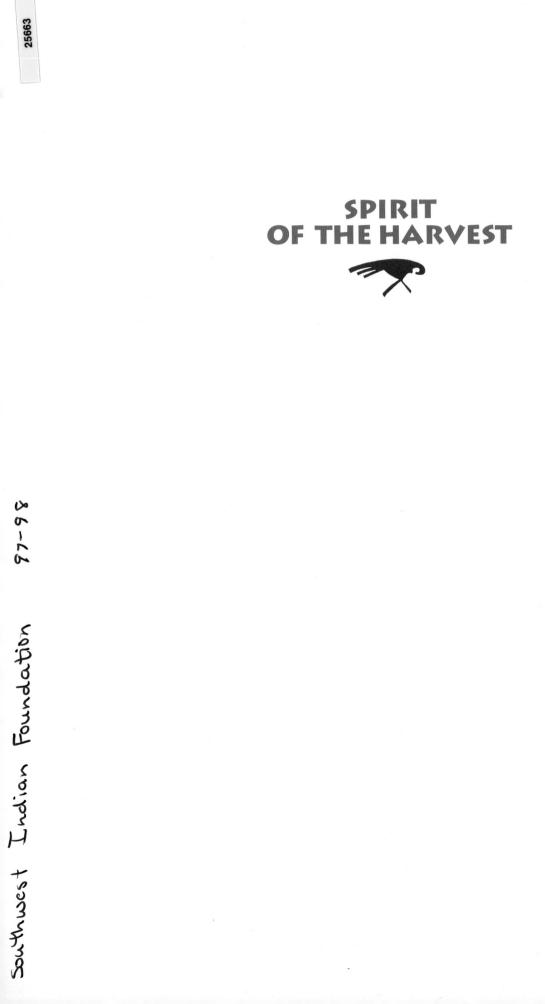

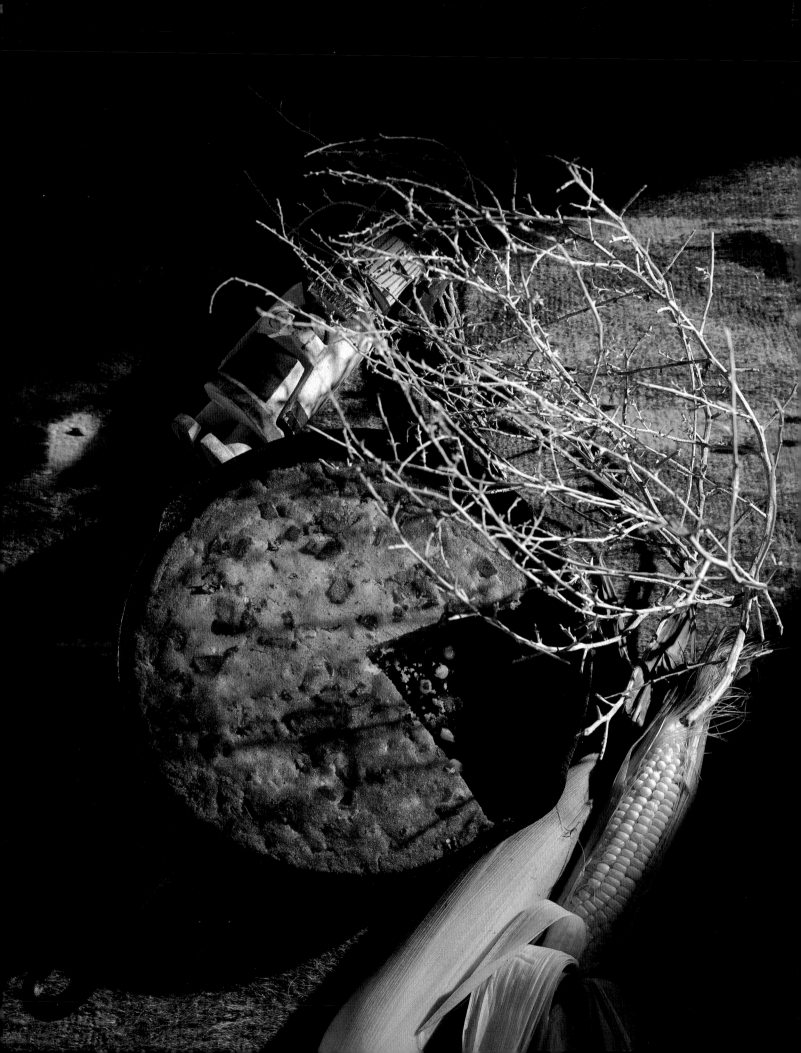

SPIRIT OF THE HARVEST

NORTH AMERICAN INDIAN COOKING

BEVERLY COX AND MARTIN JACOBS

STEWART, TABORI & CHANG
NEW YORK

Page 2: Skillet Corn Bread

Text copyright © 1991 Beverly Cox and Martin Jacobs
Photographs copyright ©1991 Martin Jacobs
The line art credits begin on page 246 and constitute
an extension of this page.
Map by Guenter Vollath
Edited by Ann ffolliott

Published in 1991 and distributed in the U.S. by
Stewart, Tabori & Chang, Inc.,
a division of U.S. Media Holdings, Inc.
575 Broadway, New York, New York 10012

Distributed in Canada by General Publishing Co. Ltd.
30 Lesmill Road, Don Mills, Ontario, Canada M3B 2T6.
Distributed in Australia and New Zealand by Peribo Pty Ltd.
58 Beaumont Road, Mount Kuring-gai, NSW 2080,
Australia. Distributed in all other territories by Grantham
Book Services Ltd., Isaac Newton Way, Alma Park Industrial
Estate, Grantham, Lincolnshire, NG31 9SD England.

Library of Congress Cataloging-in-Publication Data

Cox, Beverly, 1945–
    Spirit of the harvest- North American indian cooking/
Beverly Cox and Martin Jacobs.
            p.   cm.
    Includes index.
    ISBN 1-55670-186-1
    1. Cookery, Indian.   2. Indians in North America—Food.
3. Indians in North America—Social life and customs.
I. Jacobs, Martin.   II.Title.
TX715.C8694   1991   91-12119
641.59'297—dc20   CIP

Printed in Japan
10 9 8 7 6 5 4

THIS BOOK IS DEDICATED
TO THE FIRST AMERICANS.
THEIR CAREFUL AND CREATIVE
HUSBANDRY BROADENED THE WORLD'S
CULINARY HORIZONS WITH
SUCH IMPORTANT FOODS AS CORN,
BEANS, SQUASH, AND POTATOES,
AND THEIR ABILITY TO LIVE IN
HARMONY WITH NATURE
CONTINUES TO INSPIRE
MODERN MAN.

Wild Greens and Flowers Salad

CONTENTS

PREFACE

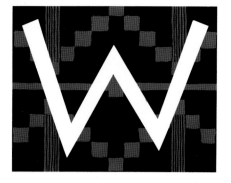

Working on *Spirit of the Harvest* has been a unique experience for us. We have both been involved with long book projects in the past, and have found that no matter how enthusiastic we were in the beginning, by the end we were glad to move on to a new subject. This book has been different. We have learned so much these past months and have met so many fascinating people that we have been reluctant to see it end. We keep hearing about recipes we would like to have included and seeing artifacts that we wish we could have photographed. Our long-standing interest in Native American food and culture has become a passion for us that can only continue.

There are many people who have made invaluable contributions to this book. First, we would like to thank our regional experts and writers: Arthur Amiotte, Oglala Lakota, artist, poet, and teacher, whose great knowledge of tribal traditions on the Great Plains was an inspiration; Dr. Clara Sue Kidwell, Professor of Native American Studies at the University of California at Berkeley, who encouraged and supported us from the beginning; and Harriet Koenig, Lecturer in Anthropology at the University of Connecticut, Stamford Campus, whose enthusiasm for this project made us feel that we were on the right path.

Our thanks go to the many wonderful people who shared with us their special knowledge of tribal foods and traditions and contributed family recipes and even hard-to-find foodstuffs from their own larders to this project: Evelyn Antelope Willow of the Northern Arapaho, Ethete, Wyoming; Helen Begay of the Navajo Nation, Los Alamos, New Mexico; the Gordon Caskey family of Lander, Wyoming; Martha Kreipe de Montaño, of the Prairie Band Potawatomi, Manager of the Information Center, National Museum of the American Indian, New York City; Martha Ferguson of the Mississippi Band of Choctaw Indians, Choctaw Museum, Philadelphia, Mississippi; Cheryl Free of the Oneida Iroquois Tribe of Wisconsin and Ron Free of the Hunkpapa Lakota, Fond du Lac, Wisconsin; Dale Old Horn of the Crow Tribe, Crow Agency, Montana; Louella Whiteman Johnson of the Crow Tribe, Lodge Grass, Montana; Barrie Kavasch, ethnobotanist and food historian, of Cherokee and Creek ancestry, Bridgewater, Connecticut, whose fine work inspired our interest in Native American cooking; Mary F. McCormick of the Sac and Fox Tribe of Oklahoma, Seminole, Oklahoma; John and Gerri McPherson, authors and teachers of primitive wilderness living skills, Randolph, Kansas; Bill Malone, Hubbell Trading Post, Ganado, Arizona; Bruce Miller of the Skokomish Tribe, Shelton, Washington; Jim Riggs, experimental archeologist, Wallowa, Oregon; Ed Sarabia, Tlingit Elder, Director of American Indian Affairs in Connecticut for the Department of Environmental Protection, Hartford, Connecticut; Bob Smith of Woodbridge, Virginia, a member of the Oneida Nation of Wisconsin; Gladys Tantaquidgeon, Mohegan Elder, Tantaquidgeon Indian Museum, Uncasville, Connecticut; Zoeanna Varret of the Houma Tribe, Du Lac, Louisiana; Mrs. George Walker of Cheyenne, Wyoming; Ed Wapp of the Comanche Tribe, Santa Fe, New Mexico; and Maralyn Yazzie of the Navajo Nation, Ganado, Arizona.

This book could never have been completed without the hard work and support of the people who assisted in typing and organization, test cooking, food styling, and tracking down elusive ingredients. Many thanks to Gretchen Barnes, who put heart and soul into this project; Shorty Caskey, who scoured Wyoming looking for chokecherries, antelope, and elk; Emily Cox; Suzanne Dale; Donna Sebro; Jane Warren; and Edna Yergin.

We would like to express our appreciation for the knowledgeable advice and enthusiastic support of the galleries and private collectors whose wonderful Native American artifacts and crafts added so much to the photographs: Harriet and Seymour Koenig were generous in every way; Louise Crowley and John Weecks of American Classics Gallery, Westport, Connecticut; Paula and Bob Eppinger, who trusted us with a family heirloom; Meridith Bjork of Canyon Road, New Canaan, Connecticut; Michael Friedman of the Friedman Gallery in Westport, Connecticut, who lent us objects from his own wonderful collection and put us in touch with many other collectors; Bill Guthman of Guthman Americana, Westport, Connecticut; Pat and Pam Guthman, Pat Guthman Antiques, Southport, Connecticut, were terrific as always; John Molloy, Historic North American Indian Art, New York City, made his collection and his knowledge readily available to us; Susan Dickerson of the Prairie's Edge, Santa Fe, New Mexico, was always enthusiastic and generous; Rolando Reyes of the Common Ground, New York City, allowed us to return to his busy store again and again; Jeff Meyers of the Primitive Arts Gallery, New York City, lent us wonderful objects from his great collection of Indian artifacts from the Northwest.

Many thanks to Linda Johnson for research and for endless patience in locating props and artifacts.

We would also like to thank our friends at Stewart, Tabori & Chang for giving us the opportunity to write this book with the best possible support: Leslie Stoker, editor-in-chief, let us find our way by following our own instincts and never held us back; Ann ffolliott, our editor, offered clear-headed advice and encouraged us to persevere, and Jim Wageman, the designer, wove all of the visual and editorial elements into a finished book that pleased us all.

—Beverly Cox and Martin Jacobs

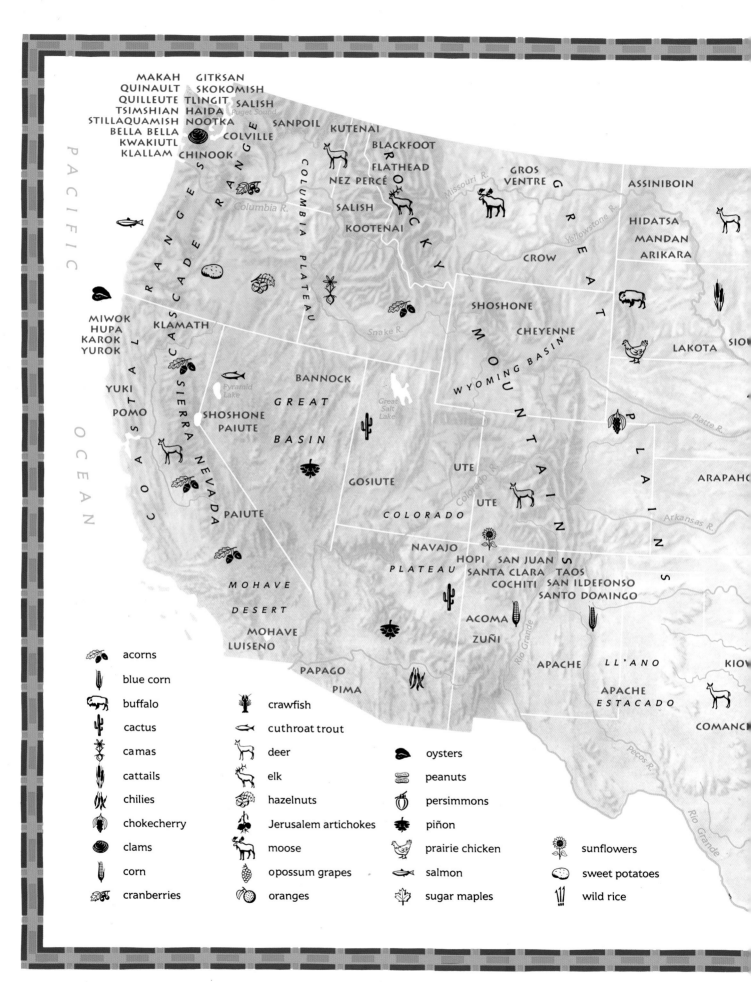

MAKAH GITKSAN
QUINAULT SKOKOMISH
QUILLEUTE TLINGIT SALISH
TSIMSHIAN HAIDA
STILLAQUAMISH NOOTKA Puget Sound SANPOIL KUTENAI
BELLA BELLA COLVILLE BLACKFOOT
KWAKIUTL FLATHEAD
KLALLAM CHINOOK NEZ PERCÉ GROS VENTRE ASSINIBOIN
SALISH HIDATSA
KOOTENAI MANDAN
ARIKARA
Columbia R.
Columbia R.
COLUMBIA PLATEAU CROW
SHOSHONE
MIWOK KLAMATH CHEYENNE LAKOTA SIOU
HUPA
KAROK Snake R.
YUROK
BANNOCK
YUKI GREAT WYOMING BASIN
POMO Pyramid SALT
Lake BASIN Great
SHOSHONE Salt ARAPAHO
PAIUTE Lake
UTE
GOSIUTE
COLORADO UTE
PAIUTE
NAVAJO
HOPI SAN JUAN
PLATEAU SANTA CLARA TAOS
MOHAVE COCHITI SAN ILDEFONSO
DESERT SANTO DOMINGO
MOHAVE ACOMA
LUISENO ZUÑI LL'ANO KIOW

PAPAGO APACHE ESTACADO
PIMA APACHE COMANC

PACIFIC OCEAN

Rio Grande Pecos R. Rio Grande

Missouri R.
Yellowstone R.
Platte R.
Colorado R.
Arkansas R.

ROCKY MOUNTAINS GREAT PLAINS
COASTAL RANGE CASCADE RANGE SIERRA NEVADA

acorns
blue corn
buffalo
cactus
camas
cattails
chilies   crawfish
chokecherry   cuthroat trout
clams   deer   oysters
corn   elk   peanuts
cranberries   hazelnuts   persimmons
                 Jerusalem artichokes piñon
                 moose   prairie chicken   sunflowers
                 opossum grapes salmon   sweet potatoes
                 oranges   sugar maples   wild rice

CHIPPEWA
(OJIBWAY)

LAKE SUPERIOR

MENOMINEE

SAC &
FOX

WINNEBAGO

INTERIOR LOWLANDS

Mississippi R.

LAKE MICHIGAN

LAKE HURON

LAKE ONTARIO

St. Lawrence R.

IROQUOIS
CONFEDERACY
MOHAWK
ONONDAGA
CAYUGA
ONEIDA
SENECA
MOHEGAN

PAUTUXET
WAMPANOAG
NARRAGANSETT

LAKE ERIE

Hudson R.

Delaware R.

DELAWARE

Missouri R.

IOWA

OMAHA
OTO

WNEE

KANSA

MISSOURI

OZARK PLATEAU

OSAGE

ROKEE

Ohio R.

APPALACHIAN MOUNTAINS

CHICAHOMINY

POWHATAN
CONFEDERACY

SHAWNEE

Tennessee R.

CHEROKEE

CATAWBA
(ESAW)

Savannah R.

COASTAL PLAIN

Mississippi R.

CHICKASAW

CREEK

QUAPAW

NATCHEZ

Red R.

CHOCTAW

CHITA

PLAIN

MICCOSUKE

COASTAL

HOUMA

ATLANTIC

OCEAN

SEMINOLE

GULF OF MEXICO

NATIVE AMERICAN FOODS

Before European contact, Indian people across North America ate food that was freshly gathered or caught, and simply prepared. Fish, fowl, and wild game were main courses. Seeds, nuts, and roots provided additional flavors and textures. Berries, fruits, and the natural sugars in tree sap and corn added sweetness.

Native cooking methods were simple. Meat, as well as other food, was boiled, roasted over an open fire, or baked in pits lined with hot coals. If wet leaves were added to the pit, the food was steamed. Seeds and nuts were eaten raw or toasted, or they were ground into meal that was used as a thickener. The meal was also mixed with water and baked into bread. Berries were mashed into sheets and dried, or they were worked into a paste with dried meat and fat, becoming a dietary staple called pemmican. Combinations of foods were simple and seasoning was minimal: a handful of wood ashes, perhaps, or a little salt, some chilies, or a few spicy tasting berries.

Indian meals were not elaborate. Generally, a single meal was served in the late morning, after everyone had risen. Food was cooked in and eaten out of a single pot, most often with the fingers. Some sort of bread was probably the only side dish, and it might have been used in place of eating utensils like forks and spoons to dip food from the pot and to sop up juices. However, food was readily available throughout the day. Pots of stew simmered slowly; handfuls of dried food could be taken for snacks. And if guests came by, they always had to be fed. Food was, and is, the common currency of hospitality in Indian communities.

Sources of food varied throughout the seasons. Periods of intense hunting or gathering resulted in substantial supplies, but storage was a problem. Meat and fish could be preserved by drying or smoking. During the buffalo-hunting season on the Plains, villages were crowded with wooden frameworks where the women hung out their strips of meat like laundry to dry in the sun. Young boys would have their fun, and prepare for their future lives as hunters and warriors, by seeing how much meat they could steal.

On the Northwest Coast, salmon and halibut fillets festooned the rafters of the longhouses. Weather permitting, halibut could be spread on the roofs of the houses to dry. Salmon, an oily fish, needed slow smoking in a small, closed hut.

For the Indians, food was more than just nourishment. Food-gathering forays were social activities for groups of women who went together to pick berries, dig roots, or collect seeds and greens. In Nevada, the piñon harvest involved virtually the whole population of Paiute villages in a period of intense activity, gathering and shelling the small, hard nuts.

Feasting was an essential part of many ceremonies. On the Great Plains, Lakota women boiled buffalo tongues for a feast during the annual Sun Dance. For the

Opposite: Cherokee Brunswick Stew

farmers of the Southwest, who depended on crops of corn, beans, and squash, ceremonies were as necessary as human labor to ensure the success of the harvest. Even today in Pueblo communities in the Southwest, corn dances are an important part of life.

Of course, many Indian people today do not live in the same areas where their ancestors did. When Europeans appeared in the New World and encountered native peoples, they introduced new ideas and new material goods that changed Indian life—brass and copper kettles for cooking, guns and metal traps for hunting. They also introduced new diseases to which the natives had no immunity, and some settlers established permanent settlements that disrupted native hunting territories or took over fallow Indian planting grounds. Many Indian groups, faced with such pressures, signed treaties giving up part or all of their land. Sometimes they received other land in exchange and were moved to new areas. The Oneida in Wisconsin, for instance, are descended from people who originally lived in upstate New York. The Choctaw tribe in Oklahoma originated in central Mississippi. The Cheyennes in Montana are probably descendants of people who once lived in the forests around the western Great Lakes. As they moved, these tribes adapted to the new foods found in their new homelands.

Virtually all contemporary American Indian cookbooks include recipes that reflect the introduction of new food sources and technologies by Europeans. Wheat flour, milk, chicken eggs, oranges, lemons, peaches, beef, and pork are only a few of these introduced foods, which are now very much a part of the diets of people in Indian communities. Nevertheless, the recipes included in this book use native foods as primary ingredients, and demonstrate the extraordinary variety of foods that were available to native people without straining the resources of the modern cook.

—Clara Sue Kidwell

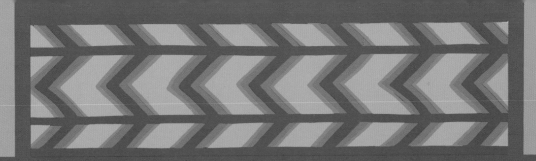

THE
SOUTHEASTERN
COAST

AND
WOODLANDS

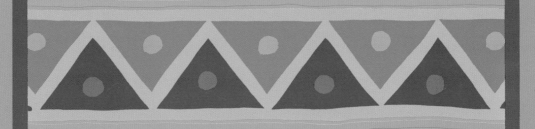

THE SOUTHEAST

America's Southeast has long been a land of rich and varied resources. The forests of the region were home to the groups of Muskogean-speaking peoples, the Choctaw, Chickasaw, Creek, and Seminole, and the Iroquoian-speaking Cherokee, who became known in history as the Five Civilized Tribes. Hernando de Soto and his soldiers found the ancestors of the Muskogean-speaking tribes raising corn near palisaded villages during their expeditions in the Southeast in the early 1540s.

Along the coastal areas, Algonquian speakers of the Powhatan Confederacy greeted the first English settlers, the colonists who attempted to settle on Roanoke Island off the coast of Virginia in 1584. From that encounter we have the earliest written and pictorial account of Indian cooking in Thomas Harriot's *A Brief and True Report of the New Found Land of Virginia*, published in 1590. The illustrations portray neatly planted fields of corn and beans inside the walls of villages and show the abundance and diversity of the creatures that were hunted or caught— deer, wild geese, gar, crabs, bass, and squid, among others.

Within the villages, men governed in public, but women controlled the household, and descent was matrilineal. Fairly well-developed class systems existed. Chiefs generally came from certain family groups. Older warriors constituted a kind of council designated the Beloved Men, while younger warriors gained status in battle. Women and children were recognized as a separate group. The Natchez amazed the French with their highly structured system of great Suns (the ruling class), nobles, and commoners (called "stinkards" by the French). The office of Sun (the highest ruler) passed through the maternal line.

Corn and beans were the main staples throughout most of the Southeast. Corn was boiled with wood ashes until the kernels swelled up into hominy. It was dried and ground into meal in wooden mortars and used to make bread, or was combined with venison and beans to make stews.

Stories about the origins of corn have a common theme among Southeastern tribes. A story from the Miccosuke in Florida and Alabama is representative. A woman feeds her family a new and delicious food that they have not seen before. Her sons wonder where she is getting it, and they secretly follow her one day to find out. They discover that she is rubbing skin from her body and forming it into little balls. She sees them and tells them that since they have discovered her secret, they must kill her and bury her body in a nearby field. The next spring, corn stalks grow from her grave. The story associates women, corn, cycles of the seasons, cycles of life and death, and fertility, and it makes corn a metaphor with many levels of meaning.

A Green Corn Ceremony was common to many Southeastern tribes. It marked not only the emergence of the new ears of corn but also the beginning of a new year. For the Creek *boskita*, people swept out their houses, put out old fires and kindled new, and visited from house to house, making up old quarrels and forgiving old grudges. The new corn symbolized a fresh start for the villagers.

The oak and hickory trees of the forests provided ample supplies of nuts. Nut meats often went into soups or stews or were ground into paste to use as a thickener. In most cases, acorns had to be leached of the bitter tannic acid they contain, but white oak acorns could be eaten raw.

Berries were also important. A Cherokee story explains the origin of strawberries: A wife left her husband because he was always quarrelsome, and she started toward the land of the Sun. Her husband was so sad that he called upon the Sun to send her back. As she walked along, the Sun caused a patch of luscious huckleberries to spring up in her path, but she ignored them. He tried a patch of blackberries, with no result, and then serviceberries. Finally, he set a patch of strawberries before her, the first that were ever created. She tried them, and as she ate she turned toward the west and began to remember her husband and miss him. She gathered a batch of berries and returned to give them to him, and he took her back.

Another spring treat was the wild onions that grew in abundance. When the Five Tribes were forced from their homes in the Southeast and relocated to Oklahoma in the 1830s, they took their food traditions with them. The Dacotah Indian Club in Muskogee, Oklahoma, put on an annual Wild Onion Dinner through the 1950s. The menu included scrambled eggs with wild onions, sassafras tea (which tastes like hot, flat root beer), "cracklin'" corn bread, and huckleberry pie. The neighboring community of Stillwell, which had a large Cherokee population, held an annual spring Strawberry Festival. The taste of the large but often woody California strawberries found in supermarkets is positively anemic beside the memory of the intensely sweet-sour tang of thimble-sized, freshly picked wild strawberries over ice cream on a warm, windy, Oklahoma spring afternoon.

—Clara Sue Kidwell

**3½ pounds stewing chicken
or rabbit parts**

3 quarts water

1 onion, chopped

1 cup chopped pecans

**Salt and ground pepper,
to taste**

**1 tablespoon minced fresh
dill (optional)**

CHEROKEE PECAN SOUP

Nuts and seeds could be the keys to survival for many Indian tribes during harsh winters. The Natchez called the full moon that occurred during the month of February, a time of scarcity, the Nut Moon. The Choctaw still make *canutchie*, a traditional preparation of hickory nuts. Dried nut meats are pounded and formed into balls that can be stored for winter. When needed, they are dissolved in water, and added to corn dishes as a thickener and flavoring, or sweetened with honey to make a nourishing drink.

In this Cherokee recipe, pecans are added for similar reasons. They give an interesting flavor to the soup, and would have stretched the pot in times when hunting was poor.

In a large stock pot, combine chicken, water, and onion. Bring to a boil. Reduce heat, cover, and simmer for 3 to 4 hours. Remove chicken from pot. When cool enough to handle, shred meat and discard skin and bones. Return meat to pot. Stir in pecans and simmer, uncovered, for 5 to 10 minutes longer. Season with salt, pepper, and dill.

Serves 6

In a heavy saucepan, combine peanuts, broth, and milk. Cook over medium heat for 5 minutes, stirring. Simmer 10 minutes longer, stirring occasionally. Sprinkle with chives and season to taste with salt and pepper. Serves 4

PEANUT SOUP

Peanuts were discovered by the Incas, who ate them, buried them with their dead, and used them as a decorative motif on pots. The Spanish conquerors of the Inca Empire took peanuts back to Europe, and from Europe they were introduced to Africa. Finally, they came back to the New World as food for the captives on Colonial slave-raiding ships. In the southeastern United States, Indians, black slaves, and white settlers ate peanuts that had been introduced from Africa. The well-traveled peanut is an important crop in the Southeast today, and is a tasty source of protein.

2 cups dry-roasted peanuts, finely chopped, or 1 cup chunky-style peanut butter
2 cups chicken broth
2 cups milk or cream
2 teaspoons snipped fresh chives
Salt and ground pepper

In a heavy saucepan, cook bacon over medium heat until crisp-tender. Pour off all but a thin film of drippings from pan. Add onion and sauté until transparent and golden. Add hominy and stir gently for 5 minutes. Remove pan from stove and reduce heat to low. Stir in buttermilk and salt and pepper. Heat soup gently for about 5 minutes, being careful not to bring it to a simmer. Sprinkle with dill. Serve warm or tepid.
Serves 4 to 6

CHOCTAW HOMINY SOUP

Hominy is an ingenious Native American method of preparing corn in which dried corn is removed from the cob and soaked in hot water mixed with wood ashes. Different varieties of corn and wood are specified in recipes from different regions, but the principle is the same. After soaking and beating with a stick the old-fashioned way (a more modern alternative is to simply boil the corn and ashes), the husks come off and the kernels puff up. The well-rinsed hominy is then boiled in fresh water until tender, or dried for later use.

This Choctaw soup is unusual. Those who like buttermilk or yogurt and hominy will be delighted, but for others it may be an acquired taste. Traditional recipes often call for salt pork, but we chose to use bacon because of its greater availability and lower salt content.

4 strips bacon, diced

½ cup chopped onion

1 cup boiled hominy,
drained (canned or frozen
hominy can be used)

2 cups buttermilk
Salt and ground pepper,
to taste

1 tablespoon chopped fresh
dill (optional)

1 pound venison or beef
  short ribs or shanks
2 quarts water
2 large onions, quartered
2 ripe tomatoes, seeded
  and diced
1 large sweet bell pepper,
  seeded and diced
1 cup fresh or frozen okra
½ cup diced potatoes
½ cup sliced carrots
½ cup fresh or frozen corn
  kernels
¼ cup chopped celery
  Salt and ground pepper,
  to taste
  Catsup, to taste

In 1540, Hernando de Soto visited the Cherokee, an offshoot of the great Iroquois Nation, and reported that they were an agricultural people who lived in log houses surrounded by well-tended fields. In the seventeenth century, the tribe established an extensive trade with early Scottish and English settlers. By 1825, forty-seven white men and seventy-three white women had married into the tribe. Sequoya, the famous inventor of the Cherokee alphabet, was the child of one of these marriages. By 1828, the Cherokee Nation was publishing its own weekly newspaper, the *Cherokee Phoenix*, and the rate of literacy among the Cherokee was higher than that of the white settlers in the region.

This Cherokee version of Pepper Pot Soup, unlike the famous pepper pots of Pennsylvania, does not call for tripe, though on some occasions it may well have been added. Also, though it is a matter of personal taste, Cherokee cooking is not extremely hot and spicy. The pepper in the pot is of the sweet bell variety.

CHEROKEE PEPPER POT SOUP

Put meat, water, and onions in a heavy soup kettle. Cover and bring to a boil over high heat. Reduce heat to low and simmer for 3 hours. Remove meat, let cool, and discard bones, returning meat to pot. Stir in remaining vegetables and simmer, partially covered, for 1½ hours. Season with salt, pepper, and catsup.
Serves 4 to 6

Scrub Jerusalem artichokes and cut into ¼-inch-thick slices. Blanch slices in boiling water for 1 minute. Drain and reserve.

Place remaining ingredients in a saucepan and bring to a boil. Pour over sliced Jerusalem artichokes and marinate for several hours, refrigerated. Serve as a condiment or as a salad on a bed of greens.
Serves 6

CHEROKEE SPICED JERUSALEM ARTICHOKES

The Jerusalem artichoke (sometimes called the sunchoke) is an ancient and still popular Indian food. This native North American tuber grows from the roots of a perennial sunflower. The plant is six- to ten-feet tall and has yellow daisy-like flowers, 2 to 3 inches in diameter. Its broad rough leaves and hairy stems make it easily recognizable. The roots are dug up in the fall, after the frost. Tribes throughout the country eat them raw and cooked in a variety of dishes.

Cherokee cooks include Jerusalem artichokes (*gu-ge*), spiced or pickled, in their impressive repertoire of relishes, pickles, jellies, and preserves. This recipe is for a small quantity and is designed to be refrigerated and eaten within a week or two.

1 pound Jerusalem artichokes

½ cup cider vinegar

¼ cup honey

½ teaspoon mustard seed

¼ teaspoon dill seed

1 tablespoon chopped fresh dill

Salt, to taste (optional)

Salad greens, for serving

4 to 5 ears fresh corn

3 tablespoons unbleached
flour

3 eggs, beaten

1 tablespoon sugar

1 teaspoon salt

¼ teaspoon ground pepper
(optional)
Dash of ground dried
spicebush berries or
allspice

2 tablespoons butter

2 cups milk

CREEK CORN PUDDING

With a sharp knife slit the rows of kernels down the length of the ears of corn. Use the back of the knife in a downward scraping motion to remove pulp. You should have about 2 cups.

Preheat oven to 325°F. In a large bowl, combine corn and flour. Beat in eggs and seasonings. In a saucepan, melt butter in milk over medium heat. Whisk hot milk into corn mixture. Pour mixture into a buttered 2-quart baking dish. Place dish in a pan of hot water and bake for 50 to 60 minutes, until custard has set. Serve as a side dish with meat or as a main course with a salad. Serves 6

Hernando de Soto, the first white man to travel through much of the Southeast, was also the first to note the number of varieties of corn that Indian people grew. Many tribes celebrated a Green Corn Ceremony annually; the Creek called it *boskita*. It was a time of thanksgiving and renewal, much as New Year's celebrations are in contemporary society. The Creek swept out the central squares of their villages, cleared out rubbish from their houses, and went from house to house visiting and settling old quarrels and grievances. They put out old fires and kindled new ones, and they feasted on green corn, which symbolized the fertility of the new corn crop.

The corn eaten during the Green Corn Ceremony was, in fact, from the immature ears of several varieties grown that resembled modern feed corn. The fresh corn we eat is usually from mature ears of sweet corn.

CORN PONES

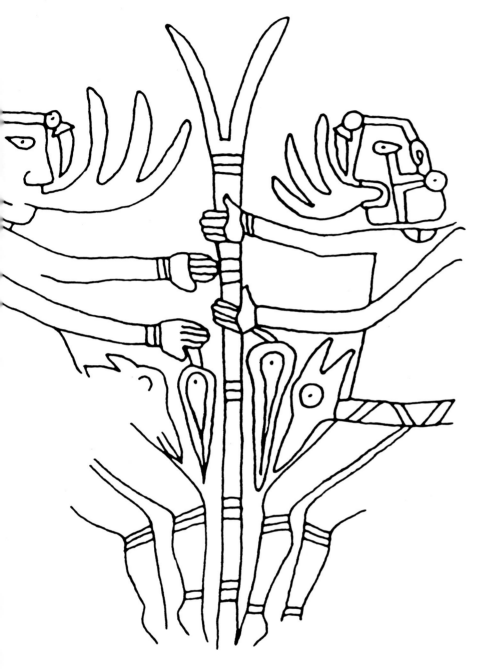

In a mixing bowl, combine cornmeal, baking powder, and salt. Stir in water and 3 tablespoons of melted bacon drippings. In a large, heavy skillet or nonstick skillet, heat enough of remaining drippings to coat the pan. Drop cornmeal batter by tablespoonfuls into the skillet. Fry pones over medium heat until browned on both sides. Serve hot.
Makes 8 to 10 pones

1½ cups cornmeal
1½ teaspoons baking powder
½ teaspoon salt (optional)
¾ cup water or milk
5 tablespoons bacon drippings, sunflower oil, or corn oil

Flat cakes or breads made from cornmeal were everyday fare for most Eastern Indian tribes. Corn pones are a particular favorite in the southeastern region. In early times they were often cooked directly in the campfire on stones, but with the introduction of the iron skillet, frying in bacon drippings became popular. More recent recipes call for substituting milk for water, but we found the water version to be very tasty, especially when served hot with butter.

**2 to 3 tablespoons bacon
   drippings, butter, or
   sunflower oil**
**2 cups boiled or canned
   hominy, drained**
**2 thinly sliced green onions
   (optional)**
**4 eggs, beaten
   Salt and ground pepper,
   to taste**

Hominy—whole, or ground for grits—is a staple of American cooking across the South. Among the Southeastern Indian tribes it is stewed, fried, baked in puddings, made into *gv-no-he-nv* (Natchez) or *gv-no-tle-nv* (Cherokee), a drink traditionally served when friends drop by, or made into hash.

HASHED HOMINY

Heat drippings in a 10-inch nonstick or well-seasoned iron skillet over medium heat. Add hominy and green onions. Sauté until lightly browned. Pour in eggs and season with salt and pepper. Stir, then allow eggs to set. Turn mixture with a pancake turner and allow to brown lightly on the other side. Serve with bacon and biscuits or corn bread for breakfast or brunch. Hashed Hominy is also a good luncheon or dinner dish if you add a watercress salad.
Serves 4

LEATHER BRITCHES BEANS

1 pound dried green beans

2 quarts water

¼ pound salt pork or slab
bacon, rind removed and
diced

Salt and ground pepper

"Leather Britches" is the colorful name of a winter dish made from dried whole green beans. Tender young beans are harvested in the summer. The ends are snapped off and the beans are strung on heavy thread and hung to dry in a sunny place for two months. The drying beans resemble britches hanging on the clothesline. When thoroughly dried, the "britches" are stored in baskets to be used all winter.

Rinse beans well. Place in a large heavy pot with water and soak for 1 hour. Add pork and bring to a boil over high heat. Reduce heat to low and simmer gently, stirring occasionally, for 3 hours, until beans are tender. Add more boiling water if necessary to keep beans from burning. Season to taste with salt and pepper. Serve with Corn Pones, Hoe Cakes, or Chippewa Bannock. Serves 4 to 6

Cherokee Mixit, like its Mediterranean cousin ratatouille, is a dish created to use the produce from a bountiful summer garden. A touch of honey and vinegar gives the vegetables a sweet-and-sour taste, reminiscent of another cousin, the caponata of Italy.

1 pound eggplant, sliced

1 pound zucchini, sliced

1 pound ripe tomatoes, peeled and seeded

1 pound sweet bell peppers, seeded and sliced.

1 pound onions, peeled and sliced

1 clove garlic, minced

3 tablespoons sunflower oil

3 tablespoons vinegar or lemon juice

2 teaspoons honey or sugar

1½ teaspoons salt

½ teaspoon ground pepper

1 to 2 teaspoons hot pepper sauce, to taste, or 1 to 2 tablespoons chopped fresh dill

In a large bowl, toss vegetables with oil, vinegar, and honey. In a heavy cooking pot or Dutch oven, layer vegetables and sprinkle with seasonings.

Place over high heat until oil begins to sizzle. Reduce heat to medium-low. Cover and simmer for about 1 hour, until vegetables are tender. Serve hot or cold. Serves 6 to 8

CHEROKEE RED AND GREEN MIXIT

NATCHEZ CORN FRITTERS

The Natchez were one of the most highly organized tribes on the lower Mississippi when the French first arrived in Louisiana in the sixteenth century. Their great village on the high bank overlooking the river was home to the "Great Sun," an absolute ruler who had power over all aspects of the lives of his subjects. A class of "nobles" constituted the warriors of the tribe, and the commoners, or "stinkards," (both terms coined by the French) were farmers and supplemented the diet of the tribe by hunting and gathering. The Natchez grew pumpkins, squash, melons, and tobacco, but corn was their principal crop and the basis of most of their cooking. French troops, with some Choctaw allies, destroyed the Natchez villages in 1730, but survivors took refuge with other tribes. Descendants of the Natchez still live among other Indian groups in small enclaves in the Southeast today.

Not much information is available about Natchez recipes, but it is assumed that their cooking was similar to that of their neighbors. This fritter recipe is typical of the tribes of this area.

4 to 5 ears fresh corn

3 eggs, well beaten

2 tablespoons cream

2 tablespoons snipped chives or thinly sliced green onions (optional)

1 teaspoon salt

3 to 4 tablespoons flour

3 to 4 tablespoons bacon drippings or corn oil

With a sharp knife, slit the rows of kernels down the length of the ears of corn. Use the back of the knife in a downward scraping motion to remove the pulp and kernels. You should have about 2 cups.

Combine corn, eggs, cream, chives, and salt in a mixing bowl. Stir in enough flour to form a thick batter.

In a heavy skillet, heat 2 tablespoons bacon drippings. Drop batter by tablespoonfuls into pan and fry for 1 to 2 minutes per side, until browned. Add more fat as needed for frying.

Makes 10 to 12 fritters

Native Americans cultivate and dry many kinds of beans. The most common varieties in the southeastern region are the navy or pea bean, black-eyed and yellow-eyed peas, and pinto, lima, and black beans. Unlike Leather Britches, these dried beans are allowed to mature in the pod until the seeds are hard. The beans are then spread out on a flat pan and dried over a low fire or in a low oven for 10 to 15 minutes. They have dried enough when they no longer stick together when you squeeze a few together in your hand. The beans are then placed in a basket or bowl, covered with a clean cloth, and stored in a warm, dry, airy place. The beans are stirred carefully every day for two weeks until no evidence of moisture remains. They are then ready to be stored in sealed (but not airtight) containers.

Bean cakes are one of many variations on the johnnycake. They are delicious when served hot with bacon and are a nourishing food to take along on hikes. We also recommend omitting the green onions and serving them hot with maple syrup.

BLACK OR WHITE BEAN CAKES

1¼ cups dried pea beans or black beans

1½ cups cornmeal

¾ cup milk or water

2 eggs, beaten

2 teaspoons salt

¼ cup thinly sliced green onions (optional)

2 to 3 tablespoons bacon drippings or sunflower oil

Soak beans overnight in cold water. Drain, rinse, and place in a large saucepan with fresh water to cover. Cook over medium heat for about 1½ hours, or until tender. Drain and reserve.

In a mixing bowl, combine cornmeal with milk, eggs, and salt. Fold in beans and green onions. Form mixture into 2- to 3-inch patties.

Heat drippings on a griddle or in a large skillet. Fry cakes for 1 to 2 minutes per side over medium heat, until golden brown. Serve hot or at room temperature.

Makes 10 to 12 cakes

Tomatoes, like many other fruits and vegetables, originated with Peruvian Indian cultures and spread north. Spanish conquistadors in Mexico found the Aztecs cultivating great fields of the fruit and carried the seeds back to Europe. Europeans were slow to eat tomatoes, though they used them as decorative plants. This prejudice spread back to the New World and persisted in parts of the United States until after the Civil War. It is not certain when Indian tribes north of Mexico first began to eat tomatoes. We do know, however, that in the Southeast there is an established Native American tradition of cooking with this versatile fruit.

We especially like this recipe for Tomato Pones and can't decide whether they are better with the addition of green onions or plain.

FRIED TOMATO PONES

2 cups peeled, seeded, and diced green or ripe tomatoes
Salt and ground pepper, to taste
1 cup cornmeal
Bacon drippings or corn oil, for frying

Place tomatoes in a mixing bowl. Season with salt and pepper. Combine tomatoes with cornmeal and form with hands into 8 pones, or patties.

Heat bacon drippings in a large skillet, over medium-high heat. Fry pones for 2 to 3 minutes on each side until golden.

Note: A nice variation of this recipe is to combine tomato mixture with ¼ cup thinly sliced green onions before forming into cakes and frying.

Makes 8 to 10 pones

**2 large sweet potatoes,
cooked and peeled**

2 eggs

½ cup unbleached flour

1 teaspoon salt

**¼ teaspoon ground, dried
spicebush berries or
allspice**

**2 to 3 tablespoons bacon
drippings, lard, or
vegetable oil**

In a mixing bowl, mash sweet potatoes. Stir in eggs, flour, and seasonings.

Heat drippings on a griddle or in a large skillet. Drop sweet potato mixture onto the griddle with a large soup spoon. Brown on one side. Turn cakes and flatten with a spatula. Brown on other side and serve hot with butter or honey.

Makes 10 to 12 cakes

The Catawba (also called the Esaw or river people) are an important Eastern tribe of the Siouan language group. They were an agricultural people who cultivated potatoes, beans, squash, and corn. Though friendly to European settlers, they engaged in fierce battles with their neighbors to the north, the Shawnee, Delaware, and Iroquois. War and smallpox severely decreased their ranks and today only a small group remains in South Carolina.

CATAWBA SWEET POTATO CAKES

1 pound carrots, peeled
  and grated
1¼ cups milk
1¼ cups unbleached flour
1¼ cups cornmeal
1½ teaspoons baking
  powder

2 eggs, beaten
2 tablespoons melted
  butter or lard
½ cup honey
½ cup dried blueberries or
  raisins

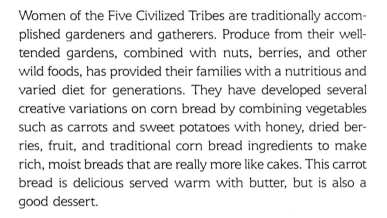

Women of the Five Civilized Tribes are traditionally accomplished gardeners and gatherers. Produce from their well-tended gardens, combined with nuts, berries, and other wild foods, has provided their families with a nutritious and varied diet for generations. They have developed several creative variations on corn bread by combining vegetables such as carrots and sweet potatoes with honey, dried berries, fruit, and traditional corn bread ingredients to make rich, moist breads that are really more like cakes. This carrot bread is delicious served warm with butter, but is also a good dessert.

CARROT BREAD

Preheat oven to 375° F. Place carrots in a saucepan, add milk, and bring to a boil. Reduce heat and simmer for 5 minutes, stirring occasionally. Remove from heat and cool.

In a mixing bowl, combine flour, cornmeal, baking powder, eggs, butter, and honey. Stir in dried blueberries or raisins, carrots, and liquid. Butter a large (5×9-inch) loaf pan. Pour batter into pan and bake for 60 to 70 minutes, until a knife inserted in the bread comes out clean.
Serves 6 to 8

Boil shucks in water for about 10 minutes, drain, and reserve. In a mixing bowl, combine cornmeal, soda, and water. Stir in black-eyed peas. Form about 4 tablespoons of the mixture into a ball and place on a corn shuck. Fold end of shuck over filling. Fold in sides and then other end to make a squared package. Tie securely with a strip of shuck.

Proceed in this fashion until all filling is used. Cook in boiling water for 45 to 50 minutes. Remove shucks and serve with butter and salt, if desired. If not serving immediately, refrigerate bread without removing the shucks. Reheat for about 10 minutes in boiling water or in a steamer before serving. Makes 8 Shuck Breads

SHUCK BREAD
(CHOCKTAW BU-NA-HA OR CHICASAW BAH-NA-HA)

We first heard about this traditional corn bread from Martha Ferguson at the Choctaw Museum in Philadelphia, Mississippi. Martha remembers her grandmother, Viola Johnson, making Shuck Bread, or *Bu-na-ha*, to serve at feasts—especially weddings. Mrs. Johnson was very strict about following the recipe exactly as it had been handed down in her family. It calls for cornmeal combined with boiling water and partially cooked black-eyed peas. Many traditional recipes also call for adding hardwood ashes to the cornmeal mixture, though today baking soda is often substituted.

There is more information about Shuck Bread in *Old Trace Cooking*, a fascinating regional cookbook written by Mrs. Gladiola B. Harris and sold at the Choctaw Museum. Mrs. Harris gives recipes for both the Choctaw (*Bu-na-ha*) and Chicasaw (*Bah-na-ha*) versions of Shuck Bread, which are quite similar. The cornmeal mixture can be cooked alone or combined with partially cooked black-eyed peas, diced sweet potato, or pumpkin. The husk-wrapped bundles are cooked in boiling water or buried in the coals and ashes around the cookpot. Mrs. Harris serves the bread with butter, not melted lard as is sometimes suggested.

8 dried or fresh corn shucks
2 cups white cornmeal
1 teaspoon baking soda
1½ cups boiling water
1 cup partially cooked black-eyed peas or frozen black-eyed peas, thawed
Butter and salt, for serving (optional)

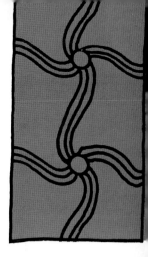

CHOCTAW ACORN BISCUITS

The Choctaw, like many other North American tribes, harvest acorns, which are gathered as soon as the shells turn brown and they begin to fall from the trees. They are then shelled like any other nut. Some sweet acorns, like those of the white oak, are good when eaten raw. Other varieties contain a bitter tannic substance that must be leached out to make them palatable.

The leaching method favored by the Choctaw is to cover freshly hulled acorns with water and bring them to a boil. Boil for 30 minutes, drain, and add fresh water. Repeat this process at least three times, or until the boiling water is a very light tea color and the bitter taste is gone. Nut meats are then dried in the sun or in a slow oven, no more than 150°F. When dried, the nut meats can be ground in a grain mill to make flour for bread or chopped into a coarser meal, as is called for in this recipe.

Preheat oven to 400°F. In a mixing bowl, combine dry ingredients. Add lard and crumble with fingertips or a pastry blender until mixture resembles coarse meal. Stir in milk. Turn dough onto a lightly floured work surface and pat out until ½ inch thick. Cut out 1½-inch biscuits. Reduce oven to 375°F. Place biscuits on a greased baking sheet and bake for 12 to 15 minutes, until golden. Serve with jelly.
Makes 10 to 12 biscuits

½ cup acorn meal
½ cup whole wheat flour
1½ teaspoons baking powder
¼ teaspoon salt (optional)
2 tablespoons lard, chilled, or 1 tablespoon each, chilled butter and vegetable shortening
About 3 tablespoons milk
Jelly

CHOCTAW FILÉ-CRAWFISH STEW

The 1929 edition of the *Picayune Creole Cookbook* contains an interesting explanation of the origin of the famous Creole gumbos of Louisiana. ". . . Filé is a powder, first manufactured by tribes of Choctaw Indians in Louisiana, from the young and tender leaves of the sassafras. The Indian squaws gathered the leaves and spread them on a stone mortar to dry. When thoroughly dried, they pounded them into a fine powder, passed them through a hair sieve, and then brought the Filé to New Orleans to sell twice a week to the famous French Market, from their reservation set aside for their home on Bayou Lacombe near Mandeville, Louisiana. The Indians used sassafras for many medicinal purposes, and the Creoles, quick to discover and apply, found the possibilities of the powdered sassafras, or filé, and originated the well-known dish, Gumbo Filé."

It appears to us that though the *Picayune* was on the right track when crediting the Choctaw with filé, it might have gone a bit further in crediting them with the invention of gumbo and the general use of powdered sassafras in cooking. If the Choctaw had not set the precedent, it is doubtful that even the intrepid Creoles would have used a medicine to thicken their stews.

¼ cup sunflower oil or
  bacon drippings
1 cup sliced green onions
½ cup chopped sweet bell
  pepper
¼ cup sliced celery
½ teaspoon dill seed
1 pound Jerusalem
  artichokes, scrubbed
  and thinly sliced

2 cups fresh or frozen
  corn kernels
1 teaspoon minced hot
  red pepper or
  1 teaspoon Louisiana
  hot sauce (optional)
5 cups water
1½ pounds live crawfish,
  well rinsed
2 to 3 teaspoons filé
  powder
  Salt (optional)
1 tablespoon minced fresh
  parsley or dill

Heat oil in a large, deep skillet or Dutch oven. Stir in green onions, bell pepper, celery, and dill seed. Cook over medium-low heat, stirring often, for about 8 minutes, until lightly browned. Add Jerusalem artichokes, corn, and hot red pepper. Sauté lightly over medium-high heat. Add water and bring to a boil. Reduce heat and simmer for about 10 minutes, or until Jerusalem artichokes are barely tender. Return to a boil over high heat, and add crawfish. Boil for 2 to 3 minutes, until they turn red. Gradually stir filé into boiling stew. Remove from heat and cover for 5 minutes. Season with salt to taste. Sprinkle with minced parsley or dill and serve immediately. Eat crawfish with your fingers and the rest with a spoon. Do not reheat or filé will turn ropey.
Serves 4 to 6

This filé gumbo recipe comes from Zoeanna Varret of the Houma Nation in Dulac, Louisiana. Louisiana and Mississippi tribes have for hundreds of years used dried, ground sassafras leaves—filé powder—as a thickener and seasoning in their soups and stews. Filé and hot peppers introduced from Mexico and the West Indies, with the French combination of flour and fat, a roux, constitute the base of the famous Cajun and Creole gumbos. Houma gumbos, made without a roux, tend to be lighter and less spicy than either the Cajun or Creole versions of the dish. According to Mrs. Varret, a Houma gumbo may also be made with crab, shrimp, and smoked sausage. She doesn't like spicy foods herself, but some Houma cooks add a good dash of Louisiana hot pepper sauce to their gumbos.

HOUMA CHICKEN FILÉ GUMBO

1 chicken (3 to 4 pounds),
   cut into serving pieces
   Salt and ground pepper
½ cup vegetable oil
2 large onions, chopped (2
   cups)
1 green bell pepper,
   chopped (1 cup)
1 quart water
1½ teaspoons filé powder
   Louisiana hot pepper
   sauce, to taste (optional)

Rinse chicken and pat dry. Season with salt and pepper and reserve. Heat oil in a large heavy pot or Dutch oven over medium heat. Add onions and bell pepper. Cook, stirring, for 10 to 12 minutes, until well browned. Pour off all but about 1 tablespoon of oil from pan and add chicken pieces. Brown chicken well on both sides, 12 to 15 minutes. If pan juices begin to stick and burn, add a few drops of water and stir and scrape with a spatula to loosen them. When chicken is browned, add remaining water. Simmer over medium-low heat for 20 to 30 minutes, until chicken is tender and cooked through. Stir in filé powder, remove from heat, and cover for 5 minutes. Season with salt, pepper, and hot sauce, if desired. Serve gumbo with rice.
Serves 4 to 6

CHEROKEE BRUNSWICK STEW

1 3½- to 4-pound rabbit, cleaned and cut into serving pieces, or 1 3½- to 4-pound chicken, cut into serving pieces

Salt and ground pepper

Cayenne pepper (optional)

4 strips bacon, diced (optional)

6 to 8 cups chicken broth or water

2 onions, peeled and quartered

2 large red potatoes, scrubbed and cubed

1 clove garlic, minced

1 bay leaf

½ teaspoon dried oregano or thyme (optional)

2 cups shelled fresh lima beans or 1 10-ounce package frozen

2 cups fresh corn kernels or 1 10-ounce package frozen

3 ripe tomatoes, quartered

2 tablespoons minced fresh parsley

Powhatan, Chicahominy, and Cherokee cooks, following Algonquian and Iroquoian custom, always had food ready to serve if someone stopped by. In their households, a bubbling pot of soup or stew simmered at all times. A favorite recipe combined wild game—usually squirrel, rabbit, or turkey—with corn, beans, and tomatoes. However, like the delicious soups produced by French farmers' wives, the exact recipe for what the Jamestown settlers called Brunswick Stew depended on what leftovers were available to add to the pot.

We like the flavor of this Cherokee version of Brunswick Stew, which calls for browning the rabbit in bacon drippings before adding broth and vegetables, but other traditional Indian recipes for the dish omit this step.

Pat rabbit pieces dry and season with salt, pepper, and cayenne. Cook bacon in a large heavy pot or Dutch oven over medium-low heat. When fat is rendered, remove bacon and reserve. Raise heat to medium-high.

Add rabbit to hot drippings and brown lightly on all sides, about 10 minutes. Add broth and bring to a boil, reduce heat, and simmer for 15 minutes. (If you omit the browning step, simmer for 30 minutes.) Add reserved bacon and remaining ingredients except parsley. Simmer for 30 to 40 minutes until meat and vegetables are tender. Taste for seasonings, adding more salt and pepper if desired. Sprinkle with parsley and serve. Serves 4 to 6

The bitter Seville orange arrived in Florida with the Spaniards in the sixteenth century. Seminole and Creek cooks, already accustomed to preparing fresh fish with grapes and other native fruits, soon adopted this exotic newcomer and made it their own.

Even today, Native American cooks often wrap food in a protective layer of grape leaves or corn husks before steaming, boiling, or baking in the ashes around a campfire. These forerunners of aluminum foil are not only effective but are also biodegradable.

SEMINOLE POMPANO STUFFED WITH ORANGES AND GRAPES

- **2 1½- to 2-pound whole pompano or red snapper, cleaned**
- **¼ teaspoon ground dried spicebush berries or allspice**
  Salt and ground pepper (optional)
- **1 small lemon**
- **2 small oranges, sliced**
- **8 to 10 black grapes, halved and seeded**
- **2 thinly sliced green onions**
- **2 tablespoons butter (optional)**
- **30 large fresh grape leaves or grape leaves in brine, rinsed**

Preheat oven to 400° F. Rub fish inside and out with seasonings. Squeeze half a lemon in and over each fish. Stuff the 2 fish with half of the orange slices, and all of the grapes and green onions. Arrange remaining orange slices on top. Place dots of butter inside and on top of fish. Wrap fish in 2 to 3 layers of slightly damp grape leaves. Secure bundles with kitchen string. Pour about 1 inch of boiling water into the bottom of a large covered roasting pan with rack. Place fish on lightly oil rack, cover, and steam in oven for 25 to 30 minutes, until fish flakes easily when thickest part is probed with a fork. Present fish on a bed of grape leaves. Serves 4 to 6

SHAWNEE SQUAW CAKE

This spicy, gingerbread-like cake is said to have been a favorite of Tenskwatawa, the Prophet, a famous Shawnee medicine man. Tenskwatawa was a brother of Tecumseh, the brilliant chief who conceived a plan to halt white expansion into Indian lands by uniting the tribes under one leader. Tecumseh was charismatic and tireless; he visited tribes from Florida to the headwaters of the Missouri, convincing even former enemies to join his union. Unfortunately, on November 7, 1811, the Prophet upset Tecumseh's plans. While his brother was away gathering support, Tenskwatawa engaged the troops of General William Henry Harrison in a premature battle at Tippecanoe in Indiana. The Indians were defeated and the union was shattered.

By the 1800s salt pork and bacon had become a part of the Indian diet, and bacon drippings and lard often replaced bear grease in cooking. Sugar, and spices such as cloves and nutmeg—though expensive—were also used. We prefer the more modern version of this recipe, which calls for vegetable shortening and milk.

Place sugar and shortening in a large heavy saucepan and heat, stirring until sugar has melted. Stir in milk, dried fruit, spices, and salt. Bring to a boil, then remove from heat and set aside to cool.

Preheat oven to 350° F. Sift dry ingredients into cooled mixture and beat to combine thoroughly. Fold in pecans and pour batter into a buttered 9½-inch springform pan. Bake for about 1 hour, or until a sharp knife inserted in center of cake comes out clean.
Serves 6 to 8

2 cups sugar

¾ cup vegetable shortening or bacon drippings

2 cups milk or water

1 cup dried, seeded wild grapes or raisins

1 teaspoon ground dried spicebush berries or allspice

1 teaspoon ground cloves

1 teaspoon ground nutmeg

½ teaspoon salt

3½ cups unbleached flour

2 teaspoons baking powder

1 teaspoon baking soda

1 cup chopped pecans or walnuts

Preheat oven to 350° F. Line the bottom of an 8 × 10-inch baking pan with bread cubes. Sprinkle currants over bread. In a mixing bowl, combine eggs, molasses, and salt. In a saucepan, bring milk to a simmer. Gradually stir milk into egg mixture. Pour mixture over bread. Place pan in a water bath. Bake for 1 hour, until most of the liquid is absorbed and pudding is lightly browned on top. Serve warm.
Serves 6

Sorghum is a cane-like grass that is also called broomcorn. For both Indians and early white settlers in the southeastern United States, sorghum molasses was a favored sweetener. Its flavor is distinctive, a bit stronger and not quite as sweet as that of cane molasses. In recipes, however, they are often used interchangeably. Demonstrations in old-fashioned sorghum-molasses making are given every Saturday, between the end of September and the end of October, at the French Camp Academy in French Camp, Mississippi, and are definitely worth seeing.

SORGHUM MOLASSES BREAD PUDDING

4 cups cubed bread (about 8 slices)
¼ cup dried currants
2 eggs, beaten
⅓ cup sorghum molasses
Pinch of salt
2 cups milk

Huckleberries and blueberries are members of the same family, but huckleberries are smaller and darker. Both berries were a major source of food for the Southeastern tribes, who ate them fresh, stewed, and cooked with meat. Large quantities were also dried for winter use.

Some early Scottish and English traders married into the leading Cherokee families and their love of baked goods is apparent in the pies, cakes, and cobblers that are very much a part of the Indian cooking of this region.

CHEROKEE HUCKLEBERRY-HONEY CAKE

½ cup butter, softened

½ cup sugar

½ cup honey

3 eggs, beaten

½ cup milk

1½ cups plus 1 tablespoon unbleached flour

2 teaspoons baking powder

⅛ teaspoon salt

1 cup fresh huckleberries or blueberries or frozen or canned berries, well drained

Preheat oven to 350° F. In a mixing bowl, cream together butter, sugar, and honey. Beat in eggs and milk. Sift in 1½ cups of flour, baking powder, and salt. Combine thoroughly. In a small bowl, toss berries with remaining flour. Gently fold berries into batter. Pour batter into a 5×9-inch loaf pan. Bake for about 1 hour, until the cake is golden brown and a knife inserted in the center comes out clean.
Serves 6 to 8

Opposite: Creek Blackberry Cobbler

Wild blackberries grow abundantly in the southeastern states. For the region's industrious Indian cooks, berry picking is a time of great bustle in the kitchen. Pies and cobblers must be baked and berries must be mashed to make juice for drinking, for jelly, and for wine. Blackberries, dewberries, huckleberries, blueberries, and grapes must be dried on racks in the sun and then stored for a cold winter's day when a bowl of steaming fruit dumplings is a welcome treat.

CREEK BLACKBERRY COBBLER

⅓ cup milk

1 egg, beaten

2 tablespoons melted butter or lard

1 teaspoon baking powder

¾ teaspoon salt

1¼ cups cornmeal

¾ cup honey

1 quart fresh or frozen blueberries

Preheat oven to 375° F. In a mixing bowl, combine milk, egg, butter, baking powder, and salt. Stir in cornmeal and ½ cup of the honey to make a batter. Place berries in the bottom of a buttered baking dish and spoon remaining honey over them. Drop batter by tablespoonfuls over berries and bake for 30 to 35 minutes, until berries are hot and bubbling and crust is golden.
Serves 6

Place grapes in a wide shallow pot or Dutch oven with enough water to cover. Bring to a boil and cook over medium heat for 6 to 8 minutes, stirring and pressing with a spoon to extract juice from grapes. Pour grapes into a large sieve over a bowl. Press out remaining juice, discard skin and seeds, and return juice to pot. You should have about 4 cups of liquid; if necessary add water. Stir in honey and set aside.

In a mixing bowl, stir together flour, sugar, baking powder, and salt. Add butter and lard and blend with your fingertips or a pastry blender until the mixture resembles a coarse meal. Using a fork, gradually stir in milk to form a soft dough. Turn dough out onto a lightly floured surface. Knead for a few seconds and roll dough out to about a ⅓-inch thickness. Cut into strips and reserve.

Over medium-high heat, return grape juice to a boil, and cook, uncovered, for about 5 minutes. Drop dough strips into boiling syrup, making sure that they are separated. Cover and reduce heat to medium-low. Simmer dumplings for 15 to 18 minutes, until dumplings are cooked through. Spoon dumplings and juices into dessert dishes. Serve topped with heavy cream or ice cream, if desired.
Serves 4 to 6

Wild grape, or "blue," dumplings are a favorite dessert of the Five Civilized Tribes. Wild opossum grapes, also called summer grapes, grow in the woods along streams throughout the southeastern states. Indian cooks gather these small black grapes and use them to make pies, jelly, and, of course, "blue" dumplings. Grapes are also dried on the stems for use in winter. When needed, the dried grapes are picked from the stems, boiled in water, and crushed. The strained juice is thickened with cornmeal and sweetened with honey to make a drink called *Oo-Ni-Na-Su-Ga Oo Ga-Me*, or boiled down to make a syrup for dumplings. The dumplings themselves are not the light fluffy puffs that we might expect. Whether dropped from a spoon or rolled out and cut into strips as suggested in this recipe, the dough has a fairly firm texture when cooked. Similar fruit dumplings are also made using blackberries and huckleberries.

WILD OPOSSUM GRAPE DUMPLINGS

8 cups fresh wild opossum grapes or other black grapes
½ cup honey
1 cup unbleached flour
1 tablespoon sugar
2½ teaspoons baking powder
¼ teaspoon salt
1 tablespoon chilled butter
1 tablespoon chilled lard or vegetable shortening
⅓ cup milk
Heavy cream or ice cream (optional)

Cut corn from the cobs and reserve for another use. Place cobs in water and bring to a boil. Cover and cook for 12 to 15 minutes. Remove cobs and strain liquid through cheesecloth or another filter. If necessary, add enough water to make 3 cups.

Place liquid in a saucepan and stir in sugar. Bring to a boil and cook until sugar is dissolved. Stir in pectin and cook 1 minute longer. Remove from heat, skim, and spoon into sterilized jars. Seal and store.
Makes 3 cups

Corn was sacred to Native Americans, and no part of it was wasted. The kernels were eaten many different ways, the husks became wrappers for Shuck Bread or dolls for the children, the stalks were used for fodder for animals, and the green cobs were made into sweet jelly and corn syrup.

This Cherokee recipe for Corn Cob Jelly comes from Rubye Alley Bumgarner of Sylva, North Carolina, who for many years owned and operated Sunset Farms, a country inn, in the foothills of the Great Smoky Mountains. She is a famous cook in the area and the author of a book, filled with wonderful stories and recipes, called *Sunset Farms, Spring Fryers Caused It All.* Her Corn Cob Jelly is light in texture and has a delicate flavor similar to apple jelly.

CHEROKEE CORN COB JELLY

12 ears fresh corn

4 cups water

4 cups sugar

1 3-fluid-ounce package
liquid fruit pectin

In a small bowl, combine brown sugar, pecans, currants, and spice. Core apples from the top, making a large enough hole in center of apple for filling but not cutting the skin at the bottom. Place 1 teaspoon of butter in each apple, followed by a tablespoon of the filling. Wrap tightly in aluminum foil and place, top down, directly in hot coals. After 5 minutes, using long tongs, turn apples right side up and continue to bake for 3 to 5 minutes longer.
Serves 4

¼ cup brown sugar

¼ cup chopped pecans

4 teaspoons dried currants
    or raisins

⅛ teaspoon ground dried
    spicebush berries,
    allspice, or cinnamon

4 baking apples

4 teaspoons butter

CHEROKEE CAMPFIRE-BAKED APPLES

The Cherokee split off from their northern kinsmen, the Iroquois, and traveled south, but they maintained many of their old traditions. The Cherokee, who were fond of apples, frequently ate them straight off the tree but also baked them. To make the dish that the Iroquois called *Wada-Gonduk* and the Cherokee called *Su-Ga-Ta*, the cookfire was brushed aside and apples were placed on the ashes. Hot embers were raked over them and the fire was rebuilt. A more modern Cherokee recipe for baking apples in a campfire, given here, is tasty and also shows how the Cherokees' cooking methods have evolved over the years as new foods were introduced into their diet.

6 large oranges

6 tablespoons honey

1 tablespoon lemon juice

Bitter Seville oranges, more like lemons than like oranges today, were brought to Florida by early Spanish expeditions in the sixteenth century as a deterrent to scurvy. Orange seeds were dropped or planted and wild orange trees became naturalized and thrived. Two hundred years later, when the naturalist William Bartram visited the Seminole, he was served oranges marinated in honey. Although modern oranges are much sweeter, they still benefit from the addition of honey. A touch of lemon juice helps to approximate the original Seminole flavor.

SEMINOLE HONEY ORANGES

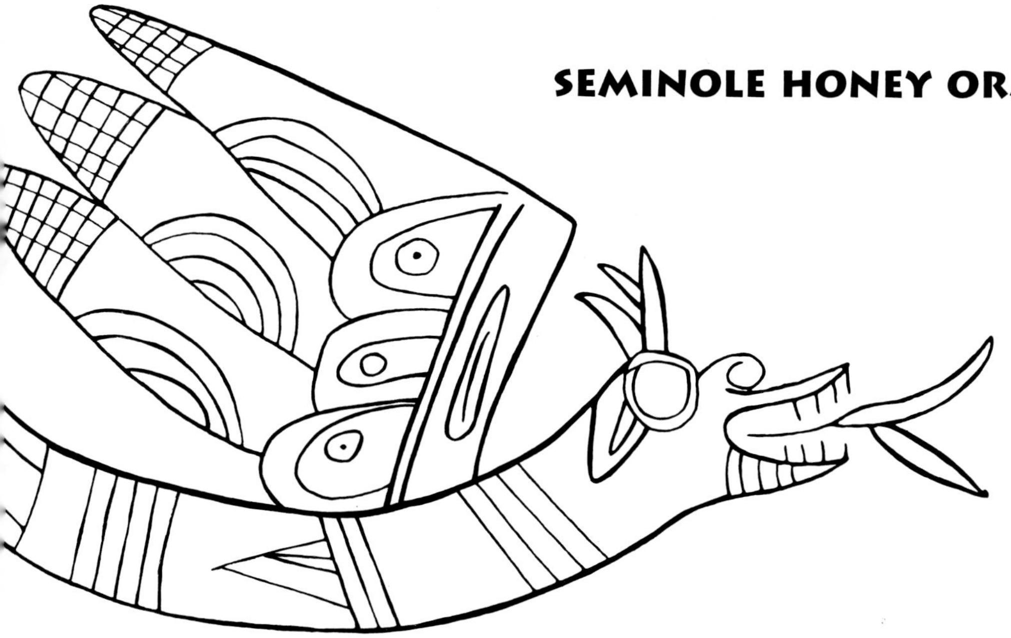

With a sharp knife, cut tops off oranges about a third of the way from the top. With a sharp knife and grapefruit spoon, carefully loosen and remove orange sections and place in a bowl. Add honey and lemon juice and toss gently. Return sections to orange shells and replace lids. Marinate oranges at room temperature for at least 4 hours before serving.
Serves 6

The native American persimmon (a corruption of the Algonquin word *pessimin*) grows wild throughout the southeastern United States. It is different in flavor and much smaller than the Oriental persimmons that appear during fall and winter months in produce markets throughout the country. In fact, there really is no substitute for this regional specialty. Both Indian tribes and European settlers in the Southeast used persimmons extensively in puddings, breads, and other confections. We were eager to include a recipe but concerned about the lack of availability of the fruit nationwide. Therefore, we were very pleased to hear about Dymple Green, of Mitchell, Indiana, whose company sells canned sweetened persimmon pulp.

This recipe comes from Lola Lively Burgess, a Choctaw woman married to a Cherokee man. The pudding is sold at their Eagle's Nest Gift Shop in Cherokee, North Carolina. As we couldn't get fresh persimmons, we used sweetened, canned pulp in this recipe and found it delicious.

CHOCTAW PERSIMMON PUDDING

8 to 12 very ripe native American persimmons or 2 cups canned, sweetened persimmon pulp (see Note)

2 eggs

1¾ cups buttermilk

2 cups sugar (see Note)

¼ cup butter, melted

2 cups unbleached flour

Heavy cream, whipped, or ice cream (optional)

Scoop fresh persimmon flesh from the skin. Discard seeds and puree flesh in a food processor or by pressing through a sieve. You will need 2 cups of pulp. Reserve. Preheat oven to 375° F. In a mixing bowl, beat eggs, then stir in buttermilk, sugar, butter, flour, and reserved persimmon. Combine thoroughly. Pour batter into a 9 × 12-inch shallow nonreactive baking dish. Bake for 35 to 45 minutes, until evenly browned on top. Cut pudding into squares and serve warm or at room temperature. Top with whipped cream or ice cream, if desired.

Note: If using canned, sweetened persimmon pulp, omit sugar in recipe.

Serves 6 to 8

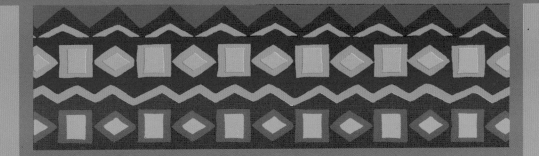

THE
NORTHEASTERN
COAST

AND
WOODLANDS

THE NORTHEAST

From the Atlantic coast to the Mississippi River and from southern Canada to the Chesapeake Bay, the traditional Indian diet before the arrival of Europeans included a wide variety of nuts, berries, seeds, roots, wild game, and seafood. Lobsters, clams, and mussels abounded in coastal areas, although lobster—such a delicacy now—was used mainly as bait when Indian men fished for bass and cod. Deer filled the woods, and flocks of turkeys gathered around Indian villages scavenging food from the kitchen middens and looking for the occasional handout. These wildfowl were a far cry from the plump, succulent Thanksgiving birds of today. They were small, very fast, and probably extremely tough, unless you got a young one.

The Northeastern coast and woodlands were inhabited by the peoples of two major language families, Iroquoian and Algonquian. The powerful Iroquois League, formed in the late sixteenth century by the great Mohawk chief Hiawatha, was composed of the Mohawk, Onondaga, Cayuga, Oneida, and Seneca. The Iroquois, who have been referred to as the Romans of the New World, were highly organized, militaristic, and politically astute. The confederacy was based in what is now New York State, but in the following two hundred years, the Iroquois expanded their sphere of influence to include all of the territory from the Ottawa River to the Tennessee River and from the Kennebec River to Lake Michigan.

The Iroquois people were hunters and farmers living in settled villages composed of bark-covered longhouses. As is true of most farming groups, their families were matrilineages. Each dwelling was home to a family group headed by a woman, which included her daughters and their spouses and her unmarried sons. Groups of related matrilineages comprised *owichiras*, and the older women in these groups selected from among their male members the sachems, or chiefs, who sat in the Grand Council of the League of the Iroquois.

The major Iroquois crops—corn, beans, and squash—were thought to be female. They were called the "Three Sisters," and Iroquois myths tell of three beautiful maidens who were often seen walking by moonlight around neighboring fields. Mohawk women planted corn in holes poked into the ground with digging sticks. When the corn had sprouted, they piled earth around the base of the stalks to discourage predators, then planted beans, whose sprouts climbed the corn stalks to reach the sun. Squash, whose broad leaves served to keep the soil moist under their shade, were sometimes planted around the base of the plants.

The lives of the Iroquois were bound up in their cycles of hunting, gathering, and farming, and the ceremonies that assured the bounty of nature. The annual ceremonial cycle began with a Maple Festival in the early spring, followed by a Planting Festival. The Strawberry Festival celebrated the small, new wild strawberries that were a particular delicacy and a harbinger of spring. Contemporary

Iroquois communities still drink wild strawberry juice at ceremonies. The Green Corn Ceremony marked the emergence of the first ears of corn. The immature "milk" corn was scraped from the cob and eaten. There was a Harvest Festival in the fall, and finally, in early February, the Midwinter Ceremony, one part of which involved the killing and cooking of a white dog.

The Algonquian language family is the most widespread of any in the United States. Although not as formally structured as the Iroquois in their alliances or their way of life, the Algonquian tribes also formed confederations. Along the northern coast, in what is now Maine and New Hampshire, the Abnaki Confederacy—made up of the Abnaki, Penobscot, Passamaquoddy, and Malecite tribes—was a very strong Algonquian block. To the south, the Delaware—another Algonquian confederacy composed of three powerful tribes known by their totem symbols as the Turtle, the Turkey, and the Wolf—controlled territories from Staten Island and Manhattan to northern Delaware. Farther west, in the woodlands around the Great Lakes, the Algonquian Chippewa, Potawamani, and Ottawa were known as the "Three Fires."

The Algonquian peoples—except in the more temperate southern areas where a settled agricultural life was possible—were hunters and gatherers who did a little farming. Family groups moved from place to place throughout the year as different foods came into season. Their wigwams were dome-shaped structures made of bent saplings covered with woven mats or bark. During the summer and fall, women gathered acorns, butternuts, hickory nuts, walnuts, grapes, chenopod seeds, Canada plums, hazelnuts, thornapples, plums, bearberries, two kinds of cherries, blackberries, blueberries, elderberries, beechnuts, sumac berries, and pepperroot. Not all these plants would be available in any one place, but they indicate the range of foods available in the woodlands. Berries were a very important part of the Northeastern diet. In one Chippewa tradition, the road to the afterlife was lined not with good intentions but with large, ripe, juicy berries that tempted the soul to stop and eat rather than continue the journey.

One of the most widely used seed plants in the area around the Great Lakes was wild rice, a kind of water grass. Various forms of water grass grow extensively throughout the Northeast in shallow lakes, but wild rice today is mostly associated with the Minnesota Chippewa. It was gathered for untold years before Europeans arrived. A French explorer, François de Crepieul, was the first European to observe its use by the Indians around Green Bay, on Lake Michigan, in 1672.

Wild rice has been called the most nutritive food consumed by the Indians of North America. It is still a dietary staple of Indian people in the Great Lakes area. It is harvested at the end of August and the beginning of September. Although wild rice has been tamed and is now grown commercially in paddies and harvested with machines, the Chippewa in Minnesota maintain that it is not the same. Many still practice the traditional way of gathering *mahnomin* (the Chippewa name for wild rice) in Minnesota lakes from canoes that are poled through the rice beds. The rice is beaten off the stems and into the canoe with wooden sticks.

The Chippewa boiled wild rice over slow fires in birchbark containers called *makuks*. (Birchbark will not burn if there is liquid in it.) The wild rice was cooked with endless combinations of ingredients—venison, fish, bear meat, wildfowl, berries, maple sugar, and animal fat—for seasoning. It could be ground into a kind of meal and used for making bread. And, like corn, it could be popped.

Wild rice continues to be important to the Chippewa people today, and both in the urban area of Minneapolis and St. Paul and in communities on the seven Chippewa reservations in Minnesota, a *Mahnomin* Festival with songs, Indian dances, and plenty of wild rice, is celebrated each fall.

Another important native food is maple sugar. The sugar maple can be found from Alabama to Lake Superior, and Indians throughout the Northeast used it to make maple sugar. Sugar maples need cold, frosty nights to develop the best sap. Sugaring begins in late winter or early spring when temperatures are warm enough to thaw the sap in the tree. A missionary to the Delaware Indians in western Pennsylvania in the late eighteenth century observed that seven to eight gallons of sap were necessary to make a pound of sugar. The sap was boiled until it reached the consistency of molasses. Then a portion of the syrup was boiled over a slow fire until it became sugar. If the hot sap was stirred until it was cold, the sugar would granulate. Usually, however, maple sugar was made into cakes in a kettle or dish and then stored in baskets. In Minnesota early in this century, Chippewa children were treated to maple sugar cakes, called "Chippewa lollipops," formed in small, round birchbark *makuks*.

Sugar-making is a time-consuming process, and an Abnaki myth from Maine explains why. Gluskabe discovered one day that the Abnaki were growing fat and lazy because they could lie under the maple trees and let the thick, rich syrup drip directly into their mouths. They refused to get up to fish or farm or hunt. Gluskabe promptly took a large bucket of water and poured it over the trees, making the sap thin and bitter. Now the people had to work hard to process the syrup to make it sweet, and they would remember to give thanks to the spirits for their food.

Wild plants provided the native tribes not only with seeds and roots but also with tender greens in the spring. Nineteenth-century accounts record that the Delaware Indians gathered the first shoots of dandelions, poke, lamb's-quarter, mustard, dock, and watercress, and parboiled them before cooking with meat.

By combining the wild game and fish and the nuts, berries, and other edible plants found in the northeastern woodlands with cultivated crops, the Indian tribes of this region provided themselves with a nutritious and balanced diet that included many foods that are much-sought-after delicacies today.

—Clara Sue Kidwell

Maple-Vinegar Marinated Racks of Venison

CLAM CHOWDER

12 cherrystone clams, rinsed
2 thick slices bacon, diced
1 cup chopped onion
3 cups chicken broth
2 cups diced new potatoes
½ teaspoon salt
¼ teaspoon ground pepper
4 to 5 ripe plum tomatoes, peeled, seeded, and diced

Although the name "chowder" comes from the French *chaudière*, the iron cauldron in which the soup was cooked, Eastern Coastal tribes made a soup combining clams and potatoes long before the arrival of Europeans. From the original recipe two versions of American clam chowder have evolved: New England-style made with cream and Manhattan-style made with tomatoes. We use the Manhattan version to take advantage of the tomato, a New World native that has contributed greatly to the world's cuisines.

Carefully shuck clams over a bowl to catch the juices. Dice clams and pour juices through a fine strainer and reserve.

In a large nonreactive saucepan, over medium heat, sauté bacon lightly. Add onion and cook until soft, about 5 minutes. Add chicken broth, clams, potatoes, salt, and pepper. Cover and simmer over low heat for 30 minutes, stirring occasionally. Add tomatoes and continue cooking 30 minutes longer. Serve hot. Serves 4 to 6

This hearty fish soup, thickened with cornmeal, is popular with both the Coastal and Woodland tribes of the Iroquois League. Traditionally, it is made from whatever saltwater or freshwater fish is most readily available. The vegetables used also vary with the season. In the spring and summer months tender young greens such as lamb's-quarter, dock, and watercress might be added and in the fall and winter months, mushrooms, dried beans, and root vegetables would take their place.

IROQUOIS SOUP (U'NEGA'GEI)

Place broth in a large saucepan. Add green onions and cornmeal. Simmer over low heat for 10 minutes. Add fish fillets, lima beans, and mushrooms. Continue cooking for 25 minutes, stirring occasionally and breaking the fish into small pieces. Add parsley and dill. Cook for 1 minute longer. Season to taste with salt and pepper and serve.
Serves 4 to 6

4 cups chicken broth

1 cup chopped green or
yellow onions

2 tablespoons cornmeal

¾ pound haddock, trout,
or bass fillets

1½ to 2 cups fresh or frozen
lima beans

4 to 6 wild mushrooms
(morels, crimini, or
shiitake), thinly sliced

2 tablespoons chopped
fresh parsley

2 tablespoons chopped
fresh dill

Salt and ground pepper

Pumpkins, squashes, and gourds are among the oldest cultivated crops of the Americas. The first two are common ingredients in the cooking of most Indian tribes that have a tradition of farming, while dried gourds have long been used as containers for water and broth. In early pumpkin soup recipes from the Northeastern Woodland Indians, the pumpkins would have been baked whole in hot ashes. The peeled and chopped pumpkin would then have been thinned with broth made from wildfowl or game, and seasoned with maple syrup and the dried and ground berries of the spicebush, a wild shrub that grows throughout the eastern woodlands. Although spicebush berries are not generally available in food stores, allspice has a similar flavor.

If using a fresh pumpkin: Preheat oven to 350°F. Place pumpkin in a baking dish and roast until easily pierced with a knife, about 1 hour. Allow pumpkin to cool. Slice off top and scoop out seeds.

Clean pumpkin fibers from seeds and discard fibers. Toss seeds with oil and salt to taste. Spread out on a baking sheet and return to oven for 15 to 20 minutes, until crisp and golden. Reserve for garnish, and for snacks.

Scrape pumpkin flesh from shell and mash, or puree if a smoother texture is desired.

Place fresh or canned pumpkin in a large saucepan and season with salt, pepper, syrup, and spicebush berry to taste. Gradually stir in enough broth to give soup a thicker or thinner consistency as desired. Simmer over medium heat for about 5 minutes, until hot. If desired, serve soup in small pumpkin or squash shells. Garnish with green onions, hazelnuts, and hulled pumpkin seeds.

Serves 4 to 6

PUMPKIN SOUP

1 small pumpkin (12 inches) or 1 29-ounce can solid-pack pumpkin

1 to 2 tablespoons peanut or sunflower oil (if using fresh pumpkin)

Salt and ground pepper

1 to 3 tablespoons maple syrup or honey

¼ to ½ teaspoon ground dried spicebush berries or allspice

3 to 4 cups chicken or beef broth

Thinly sliced green onion tops, chopped hazelnuts, and roasted pumpkin and sunflower seeds, for garnish

Indian gardeners laid out their produce gardens with an eye to beauty as well as function. Pole beans were planted next to corn for shelter, and so they could climb the corn stalks reaching for the sun. The spreading leaves of squash plants formed a ground cover that kept the soil around the plants moist and cool. Sunflowers, planted around the edges of gardens, made a pretty border and provided high-protein seeds, which were prepared in many ways.

One especially valuable variety of sunflower has delicious tuberous roots called Jerusalem artichokes or "sunchokes." When seen in the supermarket, they are sometimes mistaken for gingerroot. In fact, their flavor and texture are somewhere between those of a potato and a water chestnut. Harvested in the late fall, this very typical Indian vegetable can be eaten raw in salads or cooked like a potato.

JERUSALEM ARTICHOKE SOUP

2 pounds Jerusalem
   artichokes
6 cups chicken broth
1 cup thinly sliced green
   onions
   Salt and ground pepper
2 tablespoons minced fresh
   dill

Scrub Jerusalem artichokes and cook in simmering water for 30 to 40 minutes, until tender. Drain and discard cooking liquid. Peel and mash artichokes and place in a large saucepan. Stir in chicken broth and green onions.

Simmer for about 15 minutes. Season to taste with salt and pepper and serve sprinkled with dill.
Serves 4 to 6

SUNFLOWER SEED SOUP

Sunflower seeds predate the famous Three Sisters—corn, beans, and squash—as a staple in the cooking of Native Americans. Indian gardeners, who cultivated many varieties of sunflower, valued them both as a food—the hulled seeds are a good source of protein—and because of their beauty. Sunflower seeds were pressed to make oil and ground into butter for cooking, and the roasted seeds and hulls were brewed to make a beverage something like coffee. The seeds were also eaten out of hand as a snack and used in cooking, as in this soup recipe.

2 cups sunflower seeds, hulled

6 cups chicken broth

3 small green onions, thinly sliced

2 tablespoons chopped fresh dill

Salt and ground pepper to taste

Place sunflower seeds in a large saucepan. Add chicken broth and green onions. Cook, uncovered, over low heat for about 1 hour. Stir in dill and season with salt and pepper to taste.
Serves 4 to 6

**1 pound dried navy, kidney,
baby lima, pinto, or black
beans**

**4 to 6 strips salt pork or
thick sliced bacon**

½ cup maple syrup

½ cup molasses

1 teaspoon dry mustard

Salt (optional)

Early Algonquian and Iroquois cooks used the earth as their oven. Pots of beans flavored with maple syrup and wild mustard seed were placed in pits lined with heated stones, covered, and left to simmer for many hours. As salt pork and molasses became available they were added to the recipe and became a part of the dish as we know it today.

MAPLE-MOLASSES BAKED BEANS

Place beans in a large pot and cover them with water completely. Soak overnight. In the morning drain and cover with fresh cold water. Cook beans in liquid, over low heat, for 2 to 3 hours until tender, adding more water as needed to keep beans from sticking. Drain water from beans.

Place salt pork or bacon on the bottom and sides of a 1½-quart baking dish. In a mixing bowl, combine beans, syrup, molasses, and mustard. If using bacon, you may want to add a little salt. Pour bean mixture into baking dish and bake, covered, at 300°F. for 2 hours, stirring occasionally. Uncover and bake 30 minutes longer. Serves 6

Watercress, a member of the mustard family, grows wild in brooks throughout the United States. Native Americans gathered a variety of wild greens, including watercress, and ate them raw in salads.

Northeastern Indian tribes made vinegar from the sap of the sugar maple tree. The sap was combined with buds and twigs and left in a sunny spot to ferment, then strained through a cloth. An Indian salad dressing might combine a vinegar made from fermented maple sap with a sweetener, such as maple syrup, honey, or sugar, and oil.

2 to 3 bunches wild or
cultivated watercress
3 tablespoons cider vinegar
2 tablespoons maple syrup
¼ cup sunflower oil
1 green onion, thinly sliced

WILD WATERCRESS SALAD

Rinse watercress in 2 to 3 changes of cold water. Remove and discard tough stems. In a salad bowl, combine vinegar and syrup. Gradually whisk in oil. Add the watercress and green onion and toss lightly. Serve immediately.
Serves 4 to 6

Preheat oven to 350°F. Cut squash in half and remove seeds and strings. Pour water into a baking dish large enough to hold squash. Place halves, cut-side down, in pan. Bake for about 30 minutes, until squash starts to feel soft. Turn halves over and fill each cavity with 1 tablespoon honey and 1 teaspoon nut butter. Spread honey mixture over top edges and all over cavity.

Sprinkle lightly with spicebush berries and salt and pepper, if desired. Continue baking for 30 to 40 minutes until squash is nicely glazed. Serve with any roast meat, fowl, or game.

Serves 6

HAZELNUT-HONEY BAKED SQUASH

Nut and seed butters, made by grinding nuts or seeds into a paste, are widely used in traditional Native American Indian cooking as a spread and as a seasoning. The butter called for in this recipe may be made by chopping blanched hazelnuts or filberts in a food processor or blender until a paste is formed. If you don't wish to make your own, hazelnut butter is also available in many health and specialty food stores.

3 medium-sized acorn squash

1 cup water

6 tablespoons honey

6 teaspoons hazelnut butter

Ground dried spicebush berries or allspice

Salt and ground pepper (optional)

Succotash in its many variations is a basic Indian dish that has long been a favorite of all Americans. Among the Algonquian and Iroquian tribes of the Northeast, food—and especially succotash—was kept simmering at all times, ready for any hungry visitor or family member. We first heard of this interesting Mohegan version of the dish, in which the corn is left on the cob, at a lecture by the noted ethnobotanist and author Barrie Kavasch. She was given this recipe by Cortland Fowler, a respected elder and historian of the Mohegan tribe. After eating the corn, you have the bonus of chewing on the sweet cob. The original recipe called for bear grease instead of butter.

MOHEGAN SUCCOTASH

4 ears fresh sweet corn

3 to 4 cups fresh or 2 10-ounce packages frozen lima beans

1½ cups water

¼ cup butter

Salt and ground pepper

1⅓ cups sliced green onions

1 green and 1 red bell pepper (or 2 green), seeded and diced (optional)

With a large, sharp knife cut corn cobs into 1½-inch lengths. Place corn, beans, water, and butter with salt and pepper to taste in a large saucepan.

Cover and bring to a boil over high heat. Reduce heat to medium-low and simmer for 10 minutes. Stir in green onions and peppers and continue to simmer for 6 to 10 minutes, until beans are tender and peppers are tender-crisp. Remove lid and cook over high heat for 3 to 4 minutes, until liquid is reduced to about ½ cup. Serves 6

Water is the enemy of mushrooms, so it is best to avoid immersing them if possible. Use a soft mushroom brush or damp paper towel to wipe any dirt from the morels. Slit mushrooms down one side and if necessary wipe out the inside. If they are very sandy, rinse them in several changes of cold water and carefully pat dry. Slice morels into thin strips.

Heat oil in a large skillet over medium-high heat. Add morels and green onions. Sauté for about 1 minute. Season with salt and pepper and serve immediately.
Serves 4 to 6

½ pound fresh morels, or a combination of morels and other wild mushrooms
3 tablespoons hazelnut oil, butter, or bacon drippings
2 green onions, thinly sliced
Salt and ground pepper

ONEIDA SAUTÉED MORELS

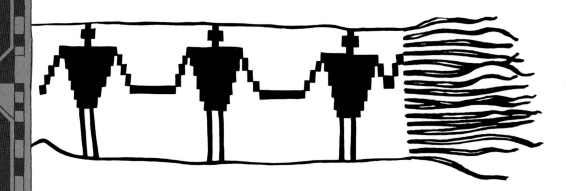

Morels are one of the wild mushrooms most coveted by gourmets, and they often have the price tag to prove it. Bob Smith, a member of the Oneida Nation, remembers gathering pounds of morels every spring for his mother, an excellent cook, who sautéed them very simply in oil or butter. The common morel is found throughout the northeastern United States. Experts say that it differs from the poisonous false morel in that its pitted oval cap is fused to its hollow stem and does not overlap like a skirt. If you are not an expert, however, we would advise eating only store-bought wild mushrooms.

HAZELNUT CAKES

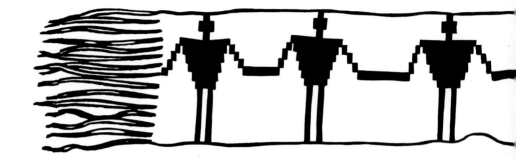

Hazelnut trees grow wild throughout the northeastern woodlands. Tribes of the region harvested the nuts and ate them either raw or roasted. Hazelnuts were also ground into flour and crushed for nut butter or oil that was used in cooking, as in the cakes below. If you can't find native hazelnuts, substitute their Asian cousins, filberts.

For the Iroquois, breakfast was the main meal of the day—indeed the only regular meal. It consisted of meat, various corn dishes, and whatever vegetables, fruits, and nuts were in season, all of which might be seasoned with maple syrup and spicy berries. We have adapted this recipe, which would be ideal for a hearty, satisfying, and leisurely Sunday brunch. Leftovers can be served as snacks for guests who drop in, much as the Iroquois kept pots of food simmering and various forms of bread ready to be eaten throughout the day as people became hungry or as guests arrived.

½ pound shelled, blanched hazelnuts

2 cups water

⅓ cup cornmeal

½ teaspoon salt

1 tablespoon maple syrup or honey

⅓ cup oil or bacon drippings, for frying

Finely chop hazelnuts. Bring water to boil in a saucepan. Add nuts to water and boil for 30 minutes, until soft. Add cornmeal, salt, and maple syrup and let stand for 30 minutes, until thick.

Heat oil in a large skillet over medium-high heat.

Drop hazelnut mixture by tablespoonfuls into skillet and brown. Turn, flatten into cakes, and brown on other side. Drain on paper towels and serve with crisp bacon and maple syrup.
Serves 4 to 6

¾ **cup wild rice, washed**

1½ **cups water**

½ **teaspoon salt**

2 **tablespoons cornmeal**

2 **to 3 tablespoons bacon
drippings or corn oil**

WILD RICE JOHNNYCAKES

Since the eighteenth century, and probably before, wild rice has played a major role in the lives of the Algonquian tribes of the Great Lakes region, both as a dietary staple and as a valuable article of barter and trade. Today, members of the Chippewa (Ojibway) and Menominee tribes harvest and process the wild rice much as their ancestors did. This recipe for Wild Rice Johnnycakes is an interesting variation on the more widely known cornmeal version of the dish. Try these cakes as an accompaniment for duck or venison, or eat them for breakfast with bacon and maple syrup.

In a medium-sized saucepan, heat rice, water, and salt. Bring to a boil and continue to boil gently for 30 to 35 minutes, until rice is just tender.

Stir in cornmeal. Allow mixture to cool. When cooled, gently mold into 8 to 10 cakes approximately 3 inches in diameter. Heat bacon drippings in a large skillet over medium heat. Add cakes and fry for 2 to 3 minutes on each side, until golden brown.

Serves 4 to 6

Preheat oven to 375° F. Bring water to a boil in a sauce-pan. Stir in cornmeal, salt, butter, and dill, if desired. Place in a buttered 8-inch square pan and bake for 25 minutes. Cut into squares and serve.

Serves 6 to 8

HOE CAKES (ALGONQUIAN NOKAKE)

Early European settlers in North America learned from the Indians to make large unleavened loaves of corn bread. The dough was spread on a board and placed beside the fire to bake. When cooked on one side, it was turned over and baked on the other side. Often the blade of a hoe was used both to prop up the board beside the fire for baking and to lean baked loaves against for an improvised cooling rack.

2 cups water

2 cups cornmeal

2 teaspoons salt

2 tablespoons butter

1 tablespoon chopped fresh dill (optional)

In a mixing bowl, combine cornmeal, water, hazelnut oil, syrup, and salt.

In a large skillet, heat 2 tablespoons oil over medium-high heat. Drop batter by tablespoonfuls into hot oil. Flatten with spatula and fry cakes until crisp and browned on both sides. Add more oil as needed.
Serves 4 to 6

CHIPPEWA BANNOCK

1½ cups cornmeal

½ cup water

4 tablespoons hazelnut oil, melted butter, or bacon drippings

4 tablespoons maple syrup or honey

½ teaspoon salt (optional)

3 to 4 tablespoons cooking oil for frying

Bannock, as a cooking term, refers to both these fried cakes, a Northwest skillet bread, and a lighter cake made with eggs and milk and flavored with molasses and spices. Simple mixtures of cornmeal and water, formed into flat cakes and fried or baked, were part of the daily fare of many Indians. Chippewa bannock is closely related to cornmeal johnny-cakes, ash cakes, and corn pones. All of these cakes, though best when eaten hot, were a practical food to take along when the tribe was on the move or warriors were out hunting.

Iroquois leaf bread made from green corn is really more a vegetable than a bread. It resembles the fresh corn tamales of Mexico and the kneel down bread of the Navajo. Although some recipes for this summer speciality call for dropping the husk packages into boiling water, we have had better results with steaming.

IROQUOIS LEAF BREAD

Shuck corn, reserving husks. Holding corn cobs upright on end, use a sharp knife to make a shallow cut down the middle of each row of kernels. Use the blade in a scraping downward motion to remove corn from cobs. In a food processor or blender, beat corn into a paste. If corn seems very liquid stir in enough cornmeal to make it easier to handle. Season with salt and pepper and reserve.

Rinse reserved husks under cold running water and pat dry. Spoon 3 to 4 tablespoons of corn paste into a large corn husk. Wrap in more husks to completely envelop paste. Tie ends with strips of husk. Continue until all paste is used. Six ears of corn should yield 12 to 15 small, tamale-like packages.

Steam leaf bread over boiling water for about 45 minutes. Allow to cool slightly before removing husks. Serve brushed with melted butter.
Serves 4 to 6

6 ears fresh sweet corn
1 to 3 tablespoons cornmeal
(optional)
Salt and ground pepper
Melted butter

4 small brook trout or chubs, about ½ pound each

½ cup coarse salt (kosher or sea)

1 cup maple sugar or brown sugar

1 teaspoon coarsely ground black pepper (optional)

½ teaspoon crushed bay leaf (optional)

2 to 3 cups maple, pecan, or hickory wood chips

To smoke fish, Eastern Woodland Indians constructed a simple tepee made of crossed sticks covered with birchbark. Fish were hung, head down, from the top of the tepee over a smoky wood fire built in a bucket or kettle below. This traditional design is still used by smoking enthusiasts today, although canvas usually replaces birchbark as the covering.

MAPLE SUGAR SMOKED FISH

Clean fish and rinse well under cold water. Mix salt, maple sugar, pepper, and bay leaf. Pat dry and rub inside and out with seasoning mixture. Place fish in a cool, dry place for about 1 hour.

Rinse fish and hang from the gills in a cool, dry, breezy place to air-dry for about 30 minutes. Place wood chips in water to soak.

If you do not have a smoker or wish to build the traditional Indian one described here, improvise by building a charcoal fire in a large covered grill with all vents open. While the fire is burning down, loop a piece of kitchen string under the

gills of each trout. Bring ends of string through the vent holes of the grill cover and tie together so that fish are suspended from lid and their tails remain at least 6 inches above coals. When coals have burned down and are covered with white ash, sprinkle a third of the damp wood chips over the fire and place lid on grill. Smoke trout for about 1 hour, adding more damp wood chips every 15 to 20 minutes to keep up smoke. Remove fish and serve hot or at room temperature. Refrigerated, the smoked fish will last about 1 week.
Serves 4 to 6

⅓ cup maple syrup

6 bluefish fillets (2½ to 3
  pounds total)

Ground dried spicebush
berries or allspice

Coarsely ground black
pepper

Salt

2 to 3 teaspoons corn oil

MAPLE-BASTED BROILED BLUEFISH

In the spring, many Northeastern tribes traveled to the Atlantic shores and bays and the rivers that flowed into them to harvest fish from the "runs" that begin in April with shad. The shad are followed in May by the voracious bluefish, which sweep along the coast eating everything in their path. Migrating fish were caught in great numbers by Indians using spears, nets, traps, and weirs. They were eaten fresh, or preserved by drying or smoking.

The dominant flavor of the fish in this recipe is complemented by the sweetness of maple syrup and the peppery seasonings. Even those who normally find bluefish too strong and oily are apt to like it when prepared this way.

Place syrup in a shallow bowl. Add fillets and turn to coat well. Sprinkle with seasonings. Lightly oil broiling rack or grill. Broil or grill fillets 5 to 6 inches from source of heat for 2 to 4 minutes on each side, basting once or twice with syrup, until fish flakes and the outside is lightly caramelized. Serve with crisp bacon, Chippewa Bannock, and Wild Watercress Salad. Serves 6

Place fish, potatoes, salt, and pepper in water to cover in a large saucepan. Cover and cook over medium heat for 25 minutes. Remove from heat and drain well. Stir in dill and mash or puree. Shape into 2- to 3-inch balls. Roll in cornmeal if a crisper crust is desired. Heat oil to 375° F. Fry codfish balls for about 1 minute, until golden brown. Remove from oil, drain well, and serve. Serves 6

CODFISH BALLS

Cod, both fresh and dried, was an important fish in the diet of Northeastern Coastal tribes. Cod was so abundant that early European settlers referred to it as "Cape Cod Turkey." Codfish balls, an old New England favorite, were originally an Indian dish. As an interesting variation on this recipe, substitute sweet potatoes for white potatoes as suggested in some early Algonquian recipes.

1½ **pounds fresh codfish**

3 **cups raw, peeled, diced**
   potatoes

2 **teaspoons salt**

½ **teaspoon ground pepper**

2 **tablespoons snipped**
   fresh dill

Cornmeal (optional)

Oil for deep frying

STOVETOP CLAMBAKE

Add water to large roasting pan with a rack and lid to just below the level of rack. Place a layer of seaweed on rack above water and add live lobsters in a single layer, if possible, with tails turned toward outer sides of pan. Sprinkle lightly with salt and add another layer of seaweed. Cover tightly and bring water to a boil. Steam for about 20 minutes until lobsters have turned bright red and small legs pull off easily. After 10 minutes of steaming, lift lid briefly and add corn.

Meanwhile, fill steamer pot (with a basket) with enough water to reach the bottom of the basket. Add a layer of seaweed to the basket. Place potatoes in basket, sprinkle lightly with salt, and top with a thin layer of seaweed. Cover pot and bring water to a boil. After 15 minutes of steaming, remove lid briefly and add clams and green onions. Cover pot and continue to steam for 6 to 8 minutes, until clams open and potatoes are tender. Serve on plates directly from pots. Melted butter for dipping is often served with clambakes today.

Note: To purge clams, place clams in seawater or salted water with a large handful of cornmeal. Refrigerate overnight. By morning, the clams should be almost sand- and grit-free.
Serves 6

Like many other American cooking traditions, we owe the clambake to early Native Americans. Tribes of the northeastern coastal region, notably the Penobscot and the Narragansett, dug pits in the sand and lined them with flat stones about the size of a man's hand. A wood fire was built on the stones. When the fire had burned down, cinders and ashes were brushed away and a thick layer of damp seaweed was placed on the red-hot stones. The pits were then filled with alternating layers of clams, potatoes, lobsters, and corn in husks, each separated by a thin layer of seaweed. Sometimes oysters, mussels, bluefish, mackerel, and small sausages wrapped in corn husks were also included. The pits were then covered with a wet animal hide or blanket weighted with stones and left to steam for about 45 minutes. The traditional method of preparing the clambake has remained much the same to this day. For the sake of those who do not own a huge clambake pot and wish to duplicate this feast in a conventional kitchen, we suggest this variation.

½ pound fresh seaweed, preferably rockweed (optional)

6 1½-pound live lobsters

1 to 2 tablespoons coarse sea salt (optional)

6 ears sweet corn, silk and outer layer of husk removed

18 to 20 small new potatoes, scrubbed but unpeeled

3 dozen clams (preferably large steamers) in shell, purged of sand and grit (see Note)

1 bunch green onions, trimmed

Melted butter for dipping (optional)

Rinse ducks and pat dry. If you want to use giblets in the stuffing, trim off tough outer layer from gizzards; thinly slice giblets and reserve. Season ducks inside and out with salt and pepper. Heat oil in a large, deep skillet over medium-high heat. Add giblets and sauté for 1 minute. Add mushrooms, onions, hazelnuts, and dill seed. Sauté for about 1 minute, until mushrooms and nuts are just golden. Add wild rice and dill to skillet. Season with salt and pepper and toss. Allow stuffing to cool. Preheat oven to 500° F. Stuff neck and body cavities of ducks loosely.

Close neck flap with a skewer and cover exposed stuffing near the tail with aluminum foil so it will stay moist. Prick skin all over with a sharp fork so that the ducks will self-baste with their fat. Reduce oven temperature to 350°F. and roast ducks, allowing about 30 minutes per pound. Prick skin and baste ducks with drippings 2 to 3 times during roasting. Ducks are done when juices run clear with no hint of pink when thigh is pierced.

Serves 6 to 8

DUCKS STUFFED WITH WILD RICE
AND WILD MUSHROOMS

According to a Chippewa legend, wild rice was first discovered when a warrior returned to his camp to find a duck sitting on the rim of his soup pot. The startled duck flew away and dropped some grain into the soup. The warrior ate the soup and found the grain to be delicious. The next morning he struck off in the direction that the duck had flown and came upon a lake where flocks of ducks were feeding on the water grass that came to be called *manomin*, or "good grain," in the Chippewa (Ojibway) tongue.

Wild ducks that feed on wild rice, such as the Blue-winged Teal, would have been used for this dish by Native American cooks. If, during hunting season, wild duck is available, by all means use it. When cooking the leaner wild ducks, tie strips of pork fat or bacon over the breasts to keep them moist when roasting. Allow only 18 to 20 minutes per pound if you prefer rare duck.

2 Long Island ducklings
(3½ to 4 pounds each)
Salt and ground pepper,
to taste

3 tablespoons hazelnut or
sunflower oil

1½ cups sliced wild
mushrooms (crimini,
shiitake, morels, or
oyster mushrooms)

1 cup sliced green onions

1 cup blanched hazelnuts

½ teaspoon dill seed

4 cups cooked wild rice

2 tablespoons chopped
fresh dill or parsley

In a saucepan, bring water and a pinch of salt to a boil. Stir in wild rice. Cover and reduce heat to low. Simmer for 50 to 60 minutes, until all water is absorbed. Fluff with a fork and reserve.

CHIPPEWA WILD RICE AND EGGS

In an 8-inch nonstick or well-seasoned skillet over medium heat, sauté bacon until crisp. Drain off all but about 2 tablespoons of drippings from skillet. Add green onions and wild rice and sauté briefly. In a mixing bowl, lightly beat eggs with ¼ teaspoon salt and pepper.

Add eggs to skillet and stir with a fork to scramble lightly. Stop stirring and allow eggs to brown lightly on the bottom. Place a large dinner plate face down on top of skillet. Carefully flip skillet and turn omelet out on plate. Slide omelet back into pan and cook for a few seconds. Cut into wedges and serve hot or at room temperature with Wild Watercress Salad.
Serves 4 to 6

1 cup water

Salt (optional)

⅓ cup wild rice, washed

4 slices bacon, cut in thin strips

4 green onions, thinly sliced

6 eggs

⅛ teaspoon ground pepper

According to one Chippewa legend, Wenebojo, the trickster, heard the grass in the lake calling to him. He made a canoe and paddled out into the lake with his grandmother, Nokomis. The grass told them it was good to eat, so Wenebojo and Nokomis tried it. The Chippewa have been eating wild rice ever since. When making this recipe, add a few sautéed morels for a delicious and elegant variation.

Wild Canada geese were plentiful in the lakes and inland waterways where the Iroquois and Algonquian Indians hunted. If, during the hunting season, a wild goose comes your way, remember that it is a leaner bird than the domestic goose called for here. When roasting a wild goose, reduce cooking time by 2 to 3 minutes per pound and cover the breast with cheesecloth soaked in oil. Baste through the cheesecloth, and remove the covering only for the last 30 minutes of cooking to allow the skin to brown.

CIDER-BASTED ROAST GOOSE

1 10- to 12-pound goose

2 tablespoons sunflower or corn oil

¾ teaspoon ground dried spicebush berries or allspice

1 quart plus 2 tablespoons water

2 cups cubed corn bread

2 cups peeled, diced apples

2 cups diced plums

1 cup thinly sliced green onions

¾ teaspoon ground ginger

Salt and ground pepper, to taste

1½ cups apple cider

4 teaspoons cornstarch

2 tablespoons cold water

Preheat oven to 450° F. Remove giblets from goose and, if necessary, pull out pin feathers and singe off hairs. Rinse with cold water and pat dry. Rub goose inside and out with oil and spicebush berries or allspice and set aside.

Place giblets in a saucepan with water and simmer over medium heat for 30 to 40 minutes until tender. Chop giblets and reserve for gravy. Reserve giblet broth.

In a mixing bowl, combine corn bread, apples, plums, and green onions. Toss with 1½ to 2 cups of reserved giblet broth. Season stuffing with ginger, salt, and pepper to taste. Stuff goose loosely and truss. Place goose, breast-side up, on a rack in a roasting pan. Reduce oven temperature to 350° F. and roast, allowing 20 to 25 minutes per pound. After 30 minutes, prick skin on sides of breast, thighs, and legs to release fat, and baste goose with cider. Continue to prick skin and baste with cider several times during roasting. Remove goose to a serving platter.

Pour pan juices into a large heat-proof measuring cup or a bowl. Skim off and discard fat. If necessary, add enough reserved giblet broth or water to pan juices to make 2 cups total liquid. Return juices to roasting pan and stir in chopped giblets. Dissolve cornstarch in cold water and stir into juices. Cook gravy over medium heat, stirring constantly, for 2 to 3 minutes until thickened. Season to taste with salt and pepper.
Serves 8

1 small turkey (10 to 12
   pounds)
2 tablespoons hazelnut or
   peanut oil
½ teaspoon ground sage
½ teaspoon ground dried
   spicebush berries or
   allspice
   Salt and ground pepper,
   to taste
1 small bunch wild onions
   or green onions
3 to 4 tablespoons honey
   A decorative string of
   cranberries and bay
   leaves or sage leaves, for
   garnish (optional)

The Pilgrims, many of them city-bred and ill-equipped for the rigors of life in the wilderness, landed at Plymouth to find an invisible feast. The sea and rivers teemed with seafood and fish, and the eastern woodlands contained abundant wildfowl and game, as well as roots, seeds, and berries. But to the untrained eye the land seemed barren and inhospitable. Without the help offered to those early settlers by Squanto (the lone survivor of the indiginous Pautuxet tribe, which had been annihilated by smallpox) and Chief Massasoit, of the neighboring Wampanoags, Thanksgiving, our most American holiday, might not be celebrated today. The wild turkeys served at the first Thanksgiving feast were probably spit-roasted; so if you have a rotisserie that will accommodate a turkey, by all means use it. Just follow these instructions and baste only during the last hour of cooking to avoid burning.

HONEY-BASTED ROAST TURKEY

Preheat oven to 350° F. Remove giblets from turkey and reserve for gravy if desired.

Rinse turkey and pat dry. Rub inside and out with oil and season with sage, spicebush berries, salt, and pepper. Stuff neck and body cavities with onions and truss, if desired. Place turkey in roasting pan. Roast, allowing 18 to 20 minutes per pound, until juices run clear with no hint of pink when thigh is pierced. During the last hour of cooking, baste turkey 2 to 3 times with honey. A good pan gravy can be made if you are pan roasting the turkey, though if you are spit roasting it you will not have the drippings.

Garnish with string of cranberries, if desired.
Serves 8 to 10

GIBLET PAN GRAVY

Turkey neck and giblets

3 cups water

2 celery tops

2 green onions

   Degreased pan juices
   from turkey

4 teaspoons cornstarch,
   dissolved in 2 tablespoons
   cold water

Salt and ground pepper

Place neck and giblets, except the liver, in a saucepan with water, celery, and green onions. Chop liver and reserve. Bring water to a boil over medium heat.

Reduce heat and simmer over medium-low heat for about 40 minutes until giblets are tender. Strain broth and reserve. Chop cooked giblets and reserve with liver. Bring 2 cups combined degreased pan juices from turkey and giblet broth to a boil. Stir in giblets and cornstarch. Cook gravy over medium heat, stirring often, until thickened. Season to taste with salt and pepper.

Maple syrup and sugar made by cooking down maple sap in bark containers suspended over a low fire were used as sweeteners by many Northeastern tribes. With the arrival of European traders, iron kettles replaced the bark containers. Combined with cranberries, maple syrup makes a delicious and easy sauce to serve with venison and fowl. For variation, add a pinch of dried ground spicebush berries or allspice.

2 cups fresh cranberries

1 cup maple syrup

1 cup water

¼ teaspoon ground dried spicebush berries or allspice (optional)

CRANBERRY-MAPLE SAUCE

In a saucepan combine cranberries, syrup, and water. Bring to a boil over medium-high heat. Reduce heat to medium-low and cook, stirring often, for about 15 minutes, until berries have burst and sauce has thickened. Stir in spicebush berry if desired. Cool and serve at room temperature. Sauce is best made several hours in advance so that flavors will blend.
Makes 2 cups

MAPLE-VINEGAR MARINATED RACKS OF VENISON

1 cup maple syrup

1 cup cider vinegar

6 juniper berries, or dried   "Frenched" and back
     spicebush berries or   bone cracked or removed
     allspice berries, crushed   for easy carving

2 racks of venison (about   2 tablespoons vegetable oil
     2½ pounds each) with   Salt and pepper, to taste
     ribs left long and   ½ pound thinly sliced bacon

Deer were plentiful throughout the northeastern wood-lands, and venison was an important food to all woodland tribes.

According to Bob Smith, a member of the Oneida Nation, Iroquois warriors believed literally that "You are what you eat." By consuming the flesh of brave or fierce animals, such as deer or bears, warriors reinforced those qualities in them-selves. Nutritionists of today acknowledge the wisdom of that ancient maxim, although their concern tends to be focused on fat and cholesterol levels. Because it is leaner than beef or lamb, venison is fast becoming the red meat of choice for many Americans.

In a large shallow bowl, combine syrup, vinegar, and crushed berries. Add venison racks, cover, and marinate, refrigerated, overnight. Turn racks 2 or 3 times. Remove venison from marinade and rub with oil. Reserve mari-nade for basting. Sprinkle venison lightly with salt and pepper. Preheat oven to 400° F. Stand racks in a shal-low oiled roasting pan just large enough to hold them and interlace the ribs to form a standing roast as pic-tured on page 57. Drape ba-con strips over the outside of the roast. If desired, cover the ends of the bones to keep them from burning. Roast for 10 minutes per pound for rare, and 12 to 13 minutes per pound for me-dium. Baste 2 to 3 times with marinade during roast-ing. Remove roast from oven and allow to stand, loosely covered, for 15 minutes be-fore carving.

To carve, cut between the first 2 chops on one side. Remove first chop and then alternate and remove the one opposite it. If carved in this manner the roast will continue to stand as you carve it.

Serves 6 to 8

4 cups milk

1 cup maple syrup

¼ cup butter

⅔ cup cornmeal

½ teaspoon dried ginger

¼ teaspoon ground nutmeg

1½ cups dried currants or raisins

Ice cream (optional)

Although today we think of it as a dessert, Indian Pudding was originally served along with meat and vegetables in late morning, as part of the main meal of the day. Early recipes call for cornmeal and dried fruit or berries, cooked with water and nut butter and sweetened with maple syrup or honey. As new ingredients became available, milk or cream often replaced water, and eggs, molasses, and more spices were added. Our version falls somewhere in the middle of this evolution and is surprisingly light and delicate.

INDIAN PUDDING

Preheat oven to 300° F. Butter a 2-quart casserole. In a saucepan, combine 3 cups of milk and the maple syrup over medium heat. Heat until just boiling and add butter. In a separate bowl, combine cornmeal, ginger, and nutmeg. Gradually stir cornmeal mixture into hot milk. Reduce heat to low and cook until thickened, about 10 minutes. Fold in currants.

Spoon mixture into the casserole. Pour remaining milk over pudding; do not stir. Bake pudding 2½ hours, or until all of the milk has been absorbed and top is golden brown. Serve warm, and top with ice cream, if desired. Serves 6

Among the Iroquois *Ha-Nun-Da-Yo*, or the Strawberry Festival, is one of the most important thanksgiving celebrations of the year. In *League of the Iroquois*, first published in 1851, Louis Henry Morgan describes a dish served during the festival. "It was concluded with a feast of strawberries. The berries were prepared with maple sugar, in capacious bark trays, in the form of jelly; and in this condition the people feasted upon this great luxury of nature." During modern observances of *Ha-Nun-Da-Yo*, strawberry juice, thinned with water, is usually served as a drink.

Native American cooks use small, flavorful wild strawberries in a variety of dishes during the short harvesting season in June and July. This bread is a traditional example.

IROQUOIS WILD STRAWBERRY BREAD

⅓ cup hazelnut butter or
    filbert butter (available
    in health food and
    gourmet stores)
1¾ cups water
½ cup honey
1 cup unbleached flour
1 cup cornmeal
1 teaspoon baking soda
1 teaspoon salt
1 cup wild strawberries or
    sliced larger berries

Preheat oven to 375° F. In a saucepan, combine nut butter and water. Bring to a boil. Remove from heat, add honey, stir, and allow to cool slightly.

In a large mixing bowl, combine flour, cornmeal, baking soda, and salt. Add nut liquid to mixture. Fold in strawberries. Bake in a greased loaf pan for 30 to 35 minutes, until a knife inserted in bread comes out clean.

Serves 6 to 8

FLUFFY CRANBERRY PUDDING

3 cups cranberry juice
½ cup maple syrup
**½ cup uncooked cream of
wheat**
**1 cup Cranberry-Maple
Sauce, page 88 (optional)**

Cranberries have long been used by Eastern Woodland tribes as a tasty and vitamin-rich addition to fall and winter dishes. As we researched cranberry recipes, we became intrigued by the combination of ingredients and cooking methods used in a recipe for cranberry pudding included in *Indian Cookin* by Herb Walker. The recipe adaptation given below produces a fluffy marshmallow-like concoction that will both please and mystify those who consume it.

Place cranberry juice and syrup in a medium-sized saucepan and bring to a boil over medium heat. Gradually add cream of wheat, stirring constantly. Reduce heat to low and cook, stirring constantly, for 10 minutes longer. Transfer to a large mixing bowl and beat for 10 minutes, until pudding has tripled in volume. Serve warm or chilled. Top with Cranberry-Maple Sauce, if desired.
Serves 6

According to folklore, one of the foods that most delighted Pilgrims at the first Thanksgiving feast was an amazing exploding grain, popcorn. For fun and as a test of skill the Indians tossed popcorn kernels into the fire and caught them in their hands as they popped. Popcorn balls made with maple syrup are an old Algonquian treat for both children and adults. They were the original Cracker Jack.

ALGONQUIAN MAPLE POPCORN BALLS

Pop corn following package instructions. Season with salt, if desired. Heat syrup and butter in a heavy saucepan over medium-high heat, stirring constantly until temperature reaches 250° F., or until a few drops form soft balls when dropped in cold water. Remove pan from heat and pour mixture over popcorn. When mixture is cool enough, toss popcorn with syrup and mold into balls, and cool on a buttered baking sheet. Store cooled popcorn balls in an airtight container.
Makes about 8

¼ cup popping corn
½ teaspoon salt (optional)
1 cup maple syrup
1½ teaspoons butter

MAPLE SYRUP CANDY

Maple "snow candy" is an early Eastern Woodland Indian treat that remains popular in Vermont to this day. There, after the syrup has been boiled to the proper consistency (crack stage), it is drizzled onto the snow and left to harden. The resulting candy is delicious, but a danger to teeth!

1½ teaspoons butter

1 cup maple syrup

Line a jelly-roll pan with aluminum foil. In a heavy saucepan, melt butter over medium-high heat. Add syrup and cook, stirring constantly, until a candy thermometer inserted in syrup reads 290° F., or until a few drops of syrup harden if placed in cold water. Place saucepan in a pan of cold water to stop cooking. Quickly pour hot syrup onto aluminum foil and allow to cool. Crack into bite-sized pieces. Place cooled candy in an airtight container and store in a cool, dry place. Makes about ⅓ pound

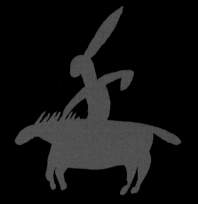

THE
GREAT PLAINS

THE GREAT PLAINS

North America's Great Plains are characterized by vast expanses of flat prairie giving way to gently rolling plains in the South. To the west are the Rocky Mountains and to the east the lakes and woodlands. Early explorers of the area called it the Great American Desert, but it was not a desert to the tribes who lived there and gleaned a variety of bountiful foods from the land and the waters. Veined with great rivers—the Missouri, the Platte, and the Mississippi—as well as numerous small creeks, the land presents a pattern of green oases amid arid plains.

The Plains are divided into three geographic regions. The Northern Plains, including the southernmost parts of Alberta, Saskatchewan, and Manitoba, were home to the Sarsi, Blackfoot, Plains Ojibway, Plains Cree, and Assiniboin. The Central Plains, consisting of eastern Colorado, Montana, Wyoming, North Dakota, South Dakota, Nebraska, and western Minnesota, were the traditional home of several large tribal groups, such as the Gros Ventre, Crow, Wind River Shoshone, Mandan, Hidatsa, Arikara, Teton Lakota, Yanktonai Dakota, Santee Dakota, Cheyenne, Omaha, Pawnee, Arapahoe, Oto, and Iowa. The Southern Plains— Kansas, Oklahoma, and Texas—were the ancestral home to the Kansa, Missouri, Osage, Jicarilla Apache, Kiowa, Kiowa Apache, Quapaw, Comanche, Wichita, and Lipan Apache.

Many Plains tribes originated in the eastern woodlands, where their traditions were agricultural. In the bottomlands along the rivers, tribes such as the Mandan, Hidatsa, Arikara, Omaha, Pawnee, and Wichita continued to grow crops, but by 1775, many of the tribes of the Central Plains had left behind their agricultural life to become equestrian bands moving about the vast plains in pursuit of the buffalo, which had become an all-important resource not only for food but also for materials for dwellings, clothing, cooking vessels, rawhide cases, and bone and horn implements. In ancient times, buffalo were killed by being driven over a precipice and after being corralled in steep-sided canyons. Carcasses that had fallen through the ice and were washed downstream by spring floods were retrieved. With the introduction of the horse, Plains Indians became skillful hunters who could shoot an arrow or bullet while pursuing a herd on horseback. (The horse, brought by Spanish explorers to New Mexico, was obtained by the tribes of the Central Plains in trade with the Comanche.)

All Plains tribes depended upon the buffalo, and methods of hunting, preservation, and preparation of the meat were similar from tribe to tribe. Those tribes that lived in permanent villages along the Missouri and other major rivers continued raising crops of corn, beans, squash, and sunflowers and ventured out onto the plains to hunt in small bands. Other tribes, such as the Lakota, moved their entire camps as they followed the large herds. The river tribes produced pottery and preferred slow cooking methods, but fragile pottery was impractical for the nomadic Plains tribes who developed other means for preserving and preparing meat. Rawhide cooking vessels were formed from the hide cut from the hump of the buffalo, which was staked over a mound of earth and left to dry in the shape of a bowl. This all-important pot was then placed in a shallow hole near the fire in the center of the lodge, close to the cooking utensils and household supplies. The pot was filled with water, and carefully selected round stones that did not shatter easily when placed in a fire were heated and transferred with wood or bone tongs to the hide pot. When the water came to a boil, the stones would cook the contents of the pot, which might include thinly sliced or diced, fresh or dried meat, wild vegetables, and tubers.

The most common way of preparing daily meals consisted of repeatedly reheating these stones and placing them in the pot. Another method was to use the cleaned paunch of a freshly killed animal suspended from upright stakes set in the ground. Inside this paunch, the cook placed water and meat, including organ meats—such as lungs, livers, kidneys, spleens, and intestines—along with the stones. This process cooked the contents and the container, which was then consumed along with the broth. Many Plains tribes used similar cooking methods; the Dakota word for the Assiniboin is translated "those who boil with stones."

Fresh meat was also roasted, and tripe and intestines containing nourishing fat were wrapped around sticks and roasted over coals much as campers roast marshmallows today. Intestines blown full of air were dried and folded into compact bundles for storage. When pieces were toasted over the fire, they became a crispy, oily treat similar to cracklings.

The mobile way of life of Plains hunters required efficiency in moving one's household belongings and food supplies, which led to many clever ways of reducing the bulk of foods by drying and compacting, such as the making of jerky. Thinly sliced meat fillets were spread and dried in the sun, then were flattened and packed in rawhide containers for future use. Another method was to bake the meat over coals and then pound it with stones into a fibrous pulp which, when mixed with bone marrow, was packed into rawhide containers that were easy to move and store. The Dakota called this basic reduction *wakapapi*, and it was the principal base for their broths. When reconstituted with a small amount of boiling water it became a hash-like meal. While we may generically call this pounded and dried meat "pemmican," it seems more appropriate to use the term for pounded, dried baked meat mixed with fresh or dried berries such as chokecherries, serviceberries, or wild currants. Pieces of pemmican were taken by warriors as rations on hunting or warring expeditions. Only small quantities were consumed at one time, as it was believed that pemmican swells inside the stomach.

While meat was the all-important staple of the Plains Indian diet, wild vegetables and berries were welcome additions. These, along with dried corn, squash, and wild rice obtained in trade with river tribes and eastern tribes, rounded out the diet. Almost all of the Plains tribes ate corn, beans, squash, and sunflowers, even after many of them became equestrian and nomadic. This attests to two seldom-recognized historical facts. First, that many of the tribes raised and traded with each other such foods in their pre-Plains days. Second, that after abandoning agriculture to pursue the buffalo, tribes regularly traded dried meat, tanned hides, and decorated garments for these vegetables with the tribes who continued to raise these foods.

Corn, beans, and squash could all be dried and reduced in bulk in a variety of ways. Corn could be left to mature on the cob in the field, gathered, and shelled, then made into hominy by boiling it with ashes. The lye in the ashes caused the hull to disintegrate and the kernel to puff up. Hominy could be eaten as such, mashed into a gruel, or sun-dried and reconstituted later. Mature dried corn could also be parched—initially in pottery containers over a fire and later in metal pots or pans. Some of it even popped. These parched kernels, made principally by the river tribes, were then further pounded in a wooden mortar with a wooden pestle or with pounding stones to reduce them to a coarse flour, which was mixed with sunflower seed flour or whole shelled nut meats, serviceberries, a little water, and hot, melted tallow or marrow. This mixture was formed into egg-shaped balls, known today as corn balls or by the Sioux as *wagmiza wasna*. Among the Mandan, Hidatsa, and Arikara, corn balls were carried by men on hunting or warring expeditions, much as nonagricultural tribes carried meat *wasna* or pemmican. On some occasions, these corn balls were traded and thus found their way into the culinary repertoire of many Plains tribes. The tradition continued once reservations were established and the hunting peoples began raising corn.

A third treatment of corn was to parboil or roast unshucked ears of green corn for ten or fifteen minutes, then remove them from the water or coals to cool. These ears, with the inner layers of husk intact, were braided into two- or three-foot strands and dried in the sun. An alternate method was to cut the kernels from the cobs and spread them in the sun to dry, which greatly reduced the bulk of the crop so that it could easily be stored or carried about. Corn prepared in this way is still used in the typical Plains corn soup; when reconstituted in liquid it swells to three times its dried state.

Beans were cooked and eaten fresh as we eat green beans today, or they were allowed to ripen and dry and were threshed. Squash and pumpkin were sliced in spirals and strung on rods to dry in the sun. Once dried they were broken into pieces and stored. Fresh squash and squash blossoms were cooked in a variety of ways, and the seeds were dried, roasted, and eaten much as is done today.

Chokecherries, serviceberries, buffalo berries, wild plums, sand cherries, yellow and black currants, wild raspberries, tiny wild strawberries, and rose hips were all gathered in their proper seasons and dried for future use and the buds of the prickly pear cactus were eaten raw in season. The typical procedure was to mash those berries that had hard pits with stones and to dry this mush into patties. The pits of wild plums were squeezed out individually by hand and the pulp dried in loose masses. The softer berries were merely dried whole and placed in sacks. These various dried berries were reconstituted with water, boiled, and thickened into a gravy-like sauce or pudding that the Dakota called *wojap*. Reconstituted berries were also added to other mixtures, including meat and corn dishes, or eaten whole. After the establishment of reservations, Plains women continued to gather and dry wild berries, but also learned to can them and to make them into jellies and jams. A favorite condiment in many contemporary houses is chokecherry syrup served with fried bread or pancakes.

Wild rice, wild turnips, cattail bulbs, wild onions, a wild potato similar to the sweet potato, lamb's-quarter, nettle leaves, the inner core of young cattail stalks, and the mushrooms that grow on box elder trees—called "tree ears" by the Dakota—are the best-known vegetables eaten by Plains Indians. Wild turnips and wild rice could be dried and saved, and the others were eaten raw in season.

Wild mint, the inner bark of the elm tree and the chokecherry tree, and the roots of wild rose bushes were gathered, saved, and used to make tea. Wild broad-leafed sage, calamus (or sweet-flag), and cedar berries were also used to make mild teas with medicinal qualities.

For the Plains tribes, as either nomadic hunters or farmers, the land gave them their sustenance and for virtually all of them, this was a very logical reason for calling her "mother." The cultivated as well as the wild, the plants and the animals, the waters and the minerals were all honored in a sacred manner. The Plains tribes today continue to revere these traditional foods and while they do not appear regularly on our tables, they are an essential element of all traditional feasting occasions, when these ancient foods serve as an important link with our ancestors.

—Arthur Amiotte

Plains turnips, *Psoralea esculenta*, are harvested in June once their flowers, purple to lavender in color, have fully blossomed. The Sioux (or Dakota) call these *tinpsila*. Two varieties are known, the round tough-skinned variety and the long and slender, tender-skinned variety called *sahiyela tinpsila* or "Cheyenne turnip." (*Sahiyela* is also the term for the flower of the *tinpsila*.) Digging turnips has traditionally been a family affair, with men helping their wives and children to gather as many as possible during the brief flowering of this plant. Originally, the Indians used sharpened sticks to dig for the roots. Since the establishment of reservations on the Plains in the 1860s and 1870s, they have used heavy sharpened crowbars.

SIOUX TURNIP AND CORN SOUP

Wild turnips, after the tough, leathery skin has been removed, are eaten raw as a special treat or they are boiled with fresh or dried meat, fresh tripe, or dried corn.

To preserve the turnips for future use, they are skinned and their stems are braided; the smaller and more delicate tubers form the first part of the braid and graduated sizes are added until the oldest, largest, and coarsest turnips form the bottom end of the braid. Servings are cut from the braid as needed. For compact storage, the raw turnips are often sliced or quartered and dried on a flat surface.

In order to use whole dried turnips in soups, you should soak them overnight, which cuts the boiling time in half. Depending on size, you can expect to boil unsoaked whole dried turnips for up to five hours before they become tender. After boiling, wild turnips resemble a boiled potato in taste and texture, but with a more earthy bouquet.

1½ pounds meaty buffalo, venison, or beef bones, cracked

6 cups meat broth or water

2 cups fresh or pre-soaked diced, dried, wild turnips or ¾ cup diced turnip, ½ cup diced rutabaga, and 1 parsnip, diced

½ cup dried corn (chicos) or 1 cup fresh or frozen corn

Salt and pepper, to taste

Place all ingredients except salt and pepper in a soup pot. Bring to a boil, reduce heat to a simmer, and skim the pot. Cover and cook for 30 to 60 minutes, until turnips and corn are tender. Shred meat from bones. Season with salt and pepper and serve hot.
Serves 6 to 8

BLACKFOOT BUFFALO AND BERRY SOUP

This recipe may have evolved when a Plains cook added a handful of pemmican to the broth to enhance its richness. The sweet dried berries in the pemmican became a tasty accent to the buffalo soup. Another possibility is that during the customary taking home of food from a feast, soup and berry pudding were mixed in the same container with delicious results.

1½ pounds buffalo or beef chuck steak, trimmed and cubed

3 tablespoons bacon drippings or vegetable oil

4 cups meat broth or water

1 cup sliced green onions

1 cup fresh serviceberries, blackberries, or blueberries, washed and drained

1 tablespoon honey
Salt and pepper, to taste

Brown meat in hot bacon drippings or oil in a Dutch oven. Add broth, green onions, berries, and honey. Simmer for 1 hour, or until meat is tender. Season with salt and pepper.
Serves 4 to 5

Wild mushrooms were gathered and eaten by many Native Americans, but on the Plains, where rainfall was erratic and agriculture was rare, they were a very special treat. Plains women and children, who knew the right mushrooms to pick, gathered several varieties, which they sautéed in fat or added to soups and stews. The remainder of the harvest was dried and stored for winter use.

4 strips bacon

¾ pound wild mushrooms—morels, chanterelles, honey mushrooms, or oyster mushrooms

¼ cup sliced green onions

Salt and pepper, to taste

SAUTÉED WILD MUSHROOMS

AND ONIONS

Cook bacon in a large skillet over medium-low heat. Remove bacon, chop or crumble, and reserve. Reserve drippings in skillet.

If they are not too sandy, wipe mushrooms with a damp cloth. If necessary, quickly rinse them in 2 to 3 changes of cold water and pat dry. (Morels should be slit up one side before rinsing as there may be sand inside the stem.) If mushrooms are large, slice them.

Heat bacon drippings over medium-high heat. Add mushrooms and green onions and sauté for 1 to 2 minutes, until just tender. Return bacon to skillet, toss, and serve. Season with salt and pepper.
Serves 4 to 6

**1½ pounds Jerusalem
artichokes (sometimes
called sunchokes)**
**2 to 3 tablespoons
vegetable oil or other
melted fat**
Salt (optional)

BROILED JERUSALEM ARTICHOKES

Plains tribes ate several varieties of wild roots and tubers. Among the most popular were arrowhead tubers (*Sagittaria lafitolia*), the source of arrowroot; wild turnips (*Psoralea esculenta*, which may be purchased in late June and July at trading posts located on or near reservations); and Jerusalem artichokes. The Jerusalem artichoke is the only one of these three that is available commercially. It has a flavor and texture that fall somewhere between those of a new potato and a water chestnut.

A popular traditional method Indians used for cooking tubers was to bury them in hot coals. They dug a small pit and lined it with stones. A wood fire was built on the stone base and was allowed to burn until only the hot embers remained. A well was made in the coals and the tubers were placed in the center and covered with more coals. This cooking technique is a good one to remember when camping, but broiling is a practical everyday alternative.

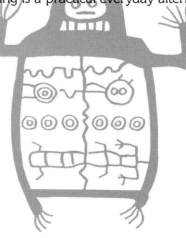

Wash Jerusalem artichokes and scrub well with a vegetable brush. Rub with oil and sprinkle lightly with salt. Broil about 6 inches from the heat for 20 to 30 minutes, or until easily pieced with a fork. Serve with meat or fish as a substitute for potatoes. Serves 6

Even before the establishment of reservations, the Plains Indians made fried bread in cast-iron pans and kettles that they had obtained in trade, and this bread continues to be very popular. One variation is cooking it in a greased cast-iron skillet over low heat and letting it gradually cook on the surface of the stove, rather than deep-frying it.

Leavening with yeast was a method learned by young women at non-Indian boarding schools after 1880, by which time many Indian houses were equipped with wood-burning cookstoves with ovens. When a feast is prepared today near the dwellings of those sponsoring it, fried yeast bread, pies, and cakes are typical fare. If the feast takes place far away in a traditional encampment, fried bread leavened with baking powder is more typical.

BLACKFOOT FRIED YEAST BREAD

The recipe below is adapted from one described by Beverly Hungry-Wolf in her fascinating book on traditional Blackfoot life, *The Ways of My Grandmothers*. Mrs. Hungry-Wolf suggests serving the bread with jam and hot chocolate on a cold winter's day. She also sometimes slits one side of the bread to form a pocket and fills it with a mixture of cooked beans, shredded cheese, and vegetables.

Place water in a mixing bowl. Sprinkle yeast over water and allow to sit for 5 minutes. Add butter, sugar, salt, and 2½ cups flour. Knead, adding enough flour to form a stiff dough. Allow to rise for 1 hour. Place oil in a deep saucepan and heat to 350°F. Form dough into disks 4 inches in diameter and about ¼ inch thick, and deep-fry for about 1 minute per side, until golden brown. Makes 8 to 10 pieces

1 cup lukewarm water

1 ¼-ounce package active dry yeast

2 tablespoons softened butter

1 tablespoon sugar

1 teaspoon salt

2½ to 3 cups unbleached flour

Deep fat, for frying

CHEYENNE BATTER BREAD

Before becoming roving buffalo hunters, the Cheyenne were an agricultural people, living in present-day Minnesota and on the Missouri River in fixed villages, where they grew corn. Their sacred rituals still reflect on how they "lost their corn" after moving to the Great Plains.

The use of cornmeal by the Cheyenne for making sophisticated corn bread variations like this one probably began in the early reservation period, when young Indian women were taught the domestic skills associated with home economics at various government and parochial boarding schools on or near reservations. These young women were taught to make breads and cakes in what was to them a new experience: a stove with an oven.

1 quart milk or water

2 cups yellow or white cornmeal

3 eggs, separated

4 tablespoons melted butter

1½ teaspoons salt

½ teaspoon pepper

Preheat oven to 375°F. Bring milk to a boil in a large saucepan over medium heat. Gradually stir in cornmeal and cook, stirring, for a few minutes until thickened. Beat in egg yolks, butter, and seasonings. In a separate bowl, beat egg whites until they stand in stiff peaks. Fold whites into corn mixture and pour into a 2-quart baking dish. Bake for 20 to 30 minutes, until puffed and golden brown on top.
Serves 6

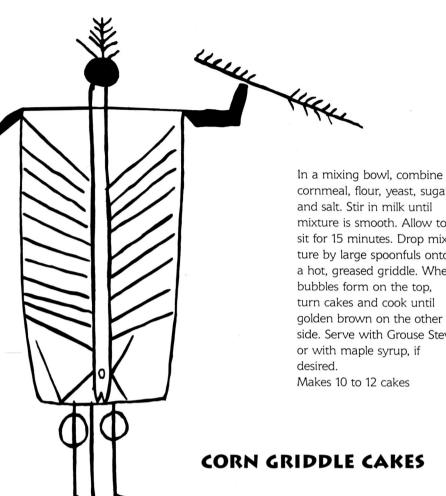

In a mixing bowl, combine cornmeal, flour, yeast, sugar, and salt. Stir in milk until mixture is smooth. Allow to sit for 15 minutes. Drop mixture by large spoonfuls onto a hot, greased griddle. When bubbles form on the top, turn cakes and cook until golden brown on the other side. Serve with Grouse Stew or with maple syrup, if desired.

Makes 10 to 12 cakes

CORN GRIDDLE CAKES

Nomadic Plains tribes carried on a regular trade with their more agriculturally inclined neighbors, and usually carried with them a supply of dried corn, which could be ground to make ash cakes, a very basic form of corn bread that was cooked in the ashes of the campfire. After reservations were established, and wheat flour, yeast, and iron griddles and frying pans became more readily available, the basic recipe evolved into more sophisticated breads and griddle cakes, as in this recipe.

2 cups cornmeal

¼ cup unbleached flour

1 ¼-ounce package active dry yeast

2 teaspoons sugar (optional)

½ to 1 teaspoon salt

1 pint milk

Maple syrup (optional)

Cattails were eaten and otherwise put to use by American Indians at all stages throughout their growing season. In the fall, the roots were dried and pounded to make a nutritious flour and the down was stripped from the mature spikes and used to stuff pillows or to line baby wrappings as a kind of disposable diaper.

The first young shoots gathered in the spring, which have a mild cucumber-like taste, are eaten raw or in salads. A short time later, the young flower stalks appear. When removed from their sheaths and boiled until tender, the flowers may be eaten from the stalk, like corn on the cob. Cattail blossoms and pollen, when combined with wheat flour, are used to make a variety of breads and pancakes such as the flapjacks described here. To harvest the blossoms, strip them from the spikes with your hands. They can be dried in a moderate oven (350°F.) and stored in an airtight container for later use. The pollen is harvested by shaking the fresh flowers over a container.

CATTAIL POLLEN FLAPJACKS

1 cup cattail pollen or flowers

1 cup whole wheat flour

2 teaspoons baking powder

½ teaspoon salt

1 egg

1 to 1¼ cups milk

1 tablespoon honey or maple syrup

4 tablespoons bacon drippings or vegetable oil

Butter and honey or syrup, for serving

Combine dry ingredients in a mixing bowl. Gradually stir in egg, milk, honey, and 2 tablespoons of drippings to make a creamy batter. Cook flapjacks until bubbles form on a hot, greased griddle or in a frying pan. Turn and cook until brown. Serve with butter and honey or syrup. Makes 10 to 12

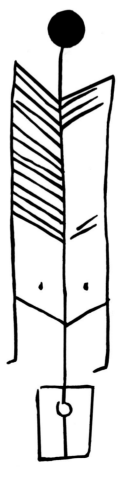

1 4- to 5-pound sugar
pumpkin

2 teaspoons salt

½ teaspoon dry mustard

1 to 2 tablespoons
vegetable oil or rendered
fat

1 pound ground venison,
buffalo, or beef

1 medium onion, chopped

1 cup wild rice, cooked

3 eggs, beaten

1 teaspoon crushed dried
sage

¼ teaspoon pepper

HIDATSA STUFFED SUGAR PUMPKIN

Many of the Plains tribes originated near the Great Lakes
and in the northern woodlands, and thus were familiar with
wild rice. It became an important trade item, finding its way
from Woodland to Prairie tribes. It was then traded for
buffalo hides and dried meat from the hunting peoples on
the Plains, who were long removed from their ancestral rice
marshes.

The Mandan and Hidatsa villages along the Missouri
River in what is now central North Dakota were major
trading centers for both indigenous and non-Indian foods.
These tribes raised pumpkins and squash and also traded
with tribes to the east and the north, and thus had a more
varied diet than their nomadic neighbors.

Preheat oven to 350°F. Cut
the top from pumpkin and
remove seeds and strings.
Prick cavity with a fork and
rub with 1 teaspoon of salt
and the mustard. Heat oil in
a large skillet. Add meat
and onion and sauté over
medium-high heat until
browned. Off the heat, stir in
wild rice, eggs, remaining
salt, sage, and pepper. Stuff
pumpkin with this mixture.
Place ½ inch of water in the
bottom of a shallow baking
pan.

Put pumpkin in the pan
and bake for 1½ hours, or
until tender. Add more water
to the pan as necessary to
avoid sticking. Cut pumpkin
into wedges, giving each
person both pumpkin and
stuffing.
Serves 6

The Cheyenne, an Algonquian tribe, were among the great buffalo hunters of the Plains. Their most important tribal ceremony was the Sun Dance, a rite of passage in which young men fasted and submitted themselves to physical torture to fulfill a vow to the Great Spirit and to prove their courage and endurance. This recipe for Buffalo Medicine Sausage is part of a more lighthearted ritual with romantic connotations. The sausage was traditionally prepared from the flesh of a virile young bull by young, unmarried warriors. The cooked sausage was placed on a bed of fresh sage, an important herb in Plains Indian ceremonies, to cool. Each young man would then take a bite of sausage and say the name of the maiden he wished to marry.

BUFFALO MEDICINE SAUSAGE

1½ pounds ground buffalo
or lean beef
Salt and pepper, to taste
About 3 yards of natural
sausage casings
2 tablespoons rendered
fat or vegetable oil
(optional)
8 ounces fresh sage

Season meat with salt and pepper and carefully stuff it into the sausage casings, taking care not to puncture the casings. Tie into 5-inch lengths. Roast sausages in a preheated 375°F. oven for 15 to 20 minutes, or fry in fat until cooked through. Place half the sage on a large piece of aluminum foil. Place sausages on top and cover with remaining sage. Wrap tightly in foil and let the sausage cool in the sage for 1½ to 2 hours.
Serves 4 to 6

Slice liver ¼ to ⅓ inch thick. In a mixing bowl, combine green onions, sage, and salt pork. Work together with a fork or a large wooden spoon until a paste is formed. Coat liver slices with paste. In a large skillet, over medium-high heat, fry liver slices in bacon drippings for 1 to 4 minutes per side until cooked to taste.
Serves 4 to 6

FRIED DEER LIVER

1½ pounds deer liver or
   beef liver
6 green onions, chopped
6 sage leaves, minced
¼ cup minced salt pork
   Bacon drippings or
   other fat, for frying

Raw buffalo, elk, and deer liver were considered a form of instant energy and were often eaten at the site of the kill by hunters exhausted after a long hunt. They did not eat the entire liver, which is a good-sized piece of meat. The remainder of the liver as well as the kidneys, which could also be eaten raw, were brought back to camp as a gift for the elderly. As a sign of respect and in deference to aged teeth, both organs were simmered until just tender and served as an especially nourishing meal. Sometimes they were fried in rendered porcupine fat.

Whether fried or boiled, these organ meats are still considered a delicacy. Be careful not to overcook them, or they will be tough.

Mix together meat, fat, vegetables, thyme, salt and pepper, and flour. Carefully stuff mixture into sausage casings, tying off 5-inch lengths.

If desired, sauté briefly in oil, just to brown. Cook in boiling water to cover for 20 minutes. Serve hot.

Serves 4 to 6

MODERN BLACKFOOT CROW GUT

(SAPOTSIS)

The Blackfoot called this sausage Crow Gut, not because it is made from a crow but because they thought it had originated with the Crow tribe. The traditional recipe, made by several Plains tribes, involves using the fatty part of the intestines of elk or buffalo and stuffing them with strips of tenderloin. When cooked, one end of the sausage is opened. Diners drink the juice or gravy from the casing and then eat the sausage itself.

This recipe is adapted from one described by Beverly Hungry-Wolf in *The Ways of My Grandmothers*, her interesting book on Blackfoot life. This modern version incorporates vegetables into the stuffing.

2 cups diced, raw elk, buffalo, or beef tenderloin

¼ cup finely chopped kidney fat or suet

3 cups diced vegetables (a combination of potatoes, carrots, turnips, and onions)

1 teaspoon dried thyme or sage
Salt and pepper, to taste

2 tablespoons unbleached flour

1½ yards natural sausage casings

1 tablespoon vegetable oil or rendered fat (optional)

PLAINS PEMMICAN

**2 cups shredded Buffalo
  Jerky (page 121) or beef
  jerky**
**1 cup chopped dried
  chokecherries or tart
  red cherries**
**6 tablespoons melted tallow
  (beef fat) or butter**

Pemmican is one of the most typical of Native American foods. The ingredients vary regionally but the basic recipe involves combining powdered dried meat or fish with melted tallow or fish oil to form a compound that can be stored in a parfleche or other dry container for long periods of time. Pemmican was carried on long overland trips and eaten when fresh game was scarce. This practical food can be added to boiling water to make a nourishing soup or eaten out of hand.

On the Plains, chokecherries or berries were often added to pemmican; they provided essential vitamin C to the vegetable-poor Plains diet. Among the Sioux, pemmican made from buffalo tenderloin combined with chokecherries and bone marrow is a sacred food. A parfleche filled with this pemmican is called a *wasna*. To receive such a parfleche or be served this sacred *wasna* is a great honor.

Combine all ingredients and form into 6 patties. Refrigerate until serving.
Serves 6

EMBER-ROASTED BUFFALO

For the Plains tribes the buffalo was all-important. These majestic animals provided the Indians with all their fundamental needs—food, clothing, and lodging—and were also central to their myths and religion.

We were interested in trying the very old cooking technique of placing meat directly on the embers, but we feared that the outside would be too burnt and the inside too raw. But by allowing 15 minutes per pound, the outside was charred—but good—and the inside a beautiful medium-rare. Threading the green onions through the roast as a seasoning technique is our innovation. It really gets the flavoring into the meat and the sliced meat with pieces of green onion in it looks attractive. Traditionally, a buffalo roast might be seasoned with wild onions, garlic, and sage.

About 3 pounds of
mesquite, or other real-
wood charcoal
1 2- to 3-pound buffalo or
beef top sirloin roast
(about 6 inches thick)
6 small green onions
1 tablespoon vegetable oil
1 teaspoon crumbled sage
Salt and pepper, to taste

Prepare a fire in a barbecue grill with the mesquite. Using a knife-sharpening steel or long narrow-bladed knife, make 6 holes—about 1 inch apart—through the roast. Push a green onion into each hole. Rub roast with oil and seasonings. When flames have died down and coals are red-hot, spread them out into a bed 2 to 3 inches wider than roast. Place roast directly on hot embers and cook for about 10 minutes per pound for very rare, or 15 minutes per pound for medium-rare. Turn roast with tongs every 3 to 4 minutes to char it on all sides. For a less-charred exterior, grill roast on a grill above the coals.
Serves 4 to 8

BUFFALO JERKY

Slice beef into strips ⅛ inch thick, 4 inches long, and 1 inch wide. Mix seasonings together and rub over meat. Lay strips on a wire rack on a baking sheet. Cook in a 150°F. oven for 8 to 10 hours, until very dry. Store in refrigerator.
Serves 6 to 8

The introduction of mass-produced salt after 1860 was a boon for jerky making. The traditional method of drying meat, as described in the chapter introduction, can take up to five days. Before salt was used in the process, it was a struggle to keep flies away from the meat during the early drying stages. When dipped in a heavy solution of salt and water, however, the thin slices of meat quickly form a dry-glazed surface unattractive to flies.

Salt was often the only seasoning in Plains jerky. The addition of chili is typical of the southwestern region and flavoring with wild ginger is most often seen in the north along the Canadian border. The oven-drying method suggested here works well, although some would argue that better flavor is obtained by the older, slower method of hanging the meat on a line over a cook stove that is kept going night and day until the meat is dried.

2 pounds buffalo or very lean beef
2 tablespoons coarse (kosher) salt
1 tablespoon ground ginger (optional)
½ to 1 teaspoon ground New Mexican red chili (optional)

The Pawnee, an agricultural people of the Caddoan language family, migrated from what is now East Texas to the area of Nebraska along the Platte River around the thirteenth century. There they established semi-permanent villages and divided their time between farming and hunting buffalo. Unlike some other Plains tribes, the Pawnee maintained this way of life even after the introduction of the horse in the late sixteenth century increased their mobility.

Prairie chickens, once abundant on the Plains, are becoming increasingly rare. For many years they were overhunted and their natural habitat has also been encroached upon by farming and by the introduction of the wild pheasant from China in the early 1900s.

2 prairie chickens or
  2 2-pound frying chickens,
  preferably free-range
  Salt and pepper, to taste
2 cups diced celery
2 cups chopped onion
3 to 4 tablespoons chopped
  fresh sage or 3 to 4
  teaspoons dried
6 tablespoons honey or
  molasses
4 medium-size sweet
  potatoes
2 tablespoons chopped
  fresh chives
1 tablespoon hulled
  sunflower seeds, lightly
  toasted

Preheat oven to 350°F. Rinse prairie chickens and pat dry. Place them in roasting pan. Season cavities with salt and pepper. Mix celery, onion, and sage together and stuff cavities. Truss birds and brush each with 1 table-spoon of honey. Roast for 20 minutes per pound, or until juices from thickest part of thigh run clear when pricked, basting occasionally with pan juices.

Scrub potatoes and prick once or twice with a fork. Roast potatoes in oven with chicken for 45 to 60 minutes, or until fork-tender. When done, slit potatoes on top and push ends in to plump open. Drizzle with remaining honey and sprinkle with chives and sunflower seeds. Season to taste with salt and pepper.

Serves 4 to 6

PAWNEE ROAST PRAIRIE CHICKEN

**2 pounds cubed moose, elk,
   deer, or lean beef**
⅓ cup maple syrup
4 cups water
Salt, to taste
3 to 4 green onions, sliced
**4 white turnips, peeled and
   diced**
**4 medium potatoes, peeled
   and diced**
1 leek, chopped

ASSINIBOIN GAME STEW

The Assiniboin, a Siouan tribe that was originally part of the Yankton, a division of the Eastern Dakota, separated from the Dakota and became bitter enemies. They allied themselves with the Cree and Chippewa in fighting the Dakota for control of the buffalo ranges. Tragically, in 1840 a smallpox epidemic wiped out most of the tribe. Today, the remaining Assiniboin live in northern Montana.

Traditionally, this stew would have been cooked using the hot stone method. Among the Plains tribes, before the introduction of iron pots, the hide or paunch of a large animal was used to line a pit in the ground or was suspended from four sticks stuck in the ground. Since a hide "pot" cannot withstand direct contact with fire, stones were heated in the campfire and placed in the stew to cook it.

Place meat on skewers and sear over an open fire or brown in a large skillet. Place browned meat and remaining ingredients in a large pot. Simmer over an open fire or on the stove over medium-low heat for about 1 hour, until meat is tender. Serves 6 to 8

Nomadic Plains tribes found dried foods like jerky and posole very practical. They were light and compact, and, with the addition of easily gathered fresh wild onions and roots, a nutritious and filling meal could be ready within a few hours of setting up camp. Jerky, of course, could be eaten while on the move to stave off hunger.

JERKY STEW

1 pound buffalo or beef jerky, coarsely diced, page 121
2 cups dried hominy, soaked at least 8 hours, or canned or frozen hominy
1½ to 2 cups chopped green onions
1 pound new or red potatoes, diced
1 teaspoon ground sage (optional)
Salt and pepper, to taste

Place jerky, dried hominy, and green onions in a large kettle. (If using canned or frozen hominy, add it during the last hour of cooking.) Cover with water and bring to a boil. Reduce heat to a simmer and cook, covered, for 2 hours, until hominy is just tender. Add potatoes, sage, and salt and pepper and cook an additional 30 to 40 minutes, until potatoes are tender. Add more water if necessary.
Serves 4 to 6

The Comanche, originally from the Great Basin and Rocky Mountains, were considered the greatest horsemen of the Plains tribes. They were buffalo hunters and fierce warriors. In early times the Comanche, along with their kinsmen the Shoshone and Kiowa, were called Snakes by other tribes because of their habit of eating snakes. As former residents of the often inhospitable terrain of the Great Basin they had learned to include reptiles and amphibians such as frogs—shunned by many Plains tribes—in their diet. These frog's legs are a treat that would satisfy a French gourmet.

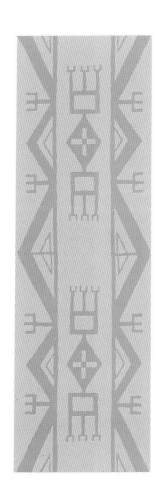

COMANCHE FRIED FROG'S LEGS

¾ cup vegetable oil

2 eggs, well beaten

1 teaspoon salt

½ teaspoon pepper

1 cup yellow cornmeal

About 1¼ cups water

3 pounds frog's legs

Heat oil in a deep skillet over medium-high heat. In a wide shallow bowl, combine eggs, salt and pepper, cornmeal, and water. Dip frog's legs in batter, making sure they are well coated. Fry in oil about 30 minutes, turning occasionally, until frog's legs are golden brown and firm to the touch.
Serves 4 to 6

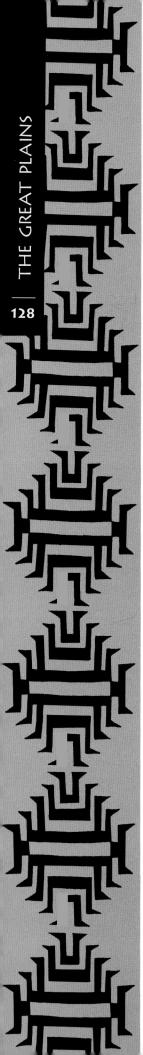

Clean and rinse trout under cold running water and slit bellies open. (If not using bacon, do not slit fish along the length of the belly; instead make 2-inch cuts at gill and vent ends and remove insides.) Rub fish inside and out with seasonings and stuff cavity with green onions. Tie bacon around fish in one or two places to hold in stuffing. Insert a sturdy, sharp-ended, forked stick in cavity and cook fish 6 to 8 inches above the campfire, or grill or broil on a lightly oiled surface for 6 to 8 minutes per side, until flesh flakes easily but is still moist and bacon is cooked.
Serves 4

4 1- to 1¼-pound whole
fresh trout
Ground dried spicebush
berries or allspice, to
taste
Salt and ground pepper
(optional)
8 green onions
4 to 8 strips thinly sliced
bacon (optional)

CAMPFIRE BROILED TROUT

The aroma and taste of trout cooked over an open fire is wonderfully appetizing. Native American cooks frequently employed the very basic cooking technique of skewering fish or small game on a spit or a forked stick fashioned from green wood and cooking it over their campfires. Green onions and ground dried spicebush berries, similar to allspice, are traditional native seasonings. Salt pork and bacon, introduced by European traders and settlers, eventually became popular as a fat for frying and flavoring other meats and fish.

GROUSE STEWED WITH GREENS

Several members of the grouse family are found on the Great Plains. The sharp-tailed grouse—slightly smaller than a female pheasant, which it resembles—is very good eating. The blue grouse, found mostly around the Rocky Mountains, feeds on insects and berries in summer, and on pine needles during the winter months. The handsome ruffed grouse, so called because of the ruff of feathers around its neck, is smaller. Sage grouse, the largest, may weigh as much as 4 pounds. They feed on the buds and leaves of sagebrush and are best if eaten young, as the herb strongly flavors the flesh of the mature birds.

2 dressed grouse or Cornish hens

4 tablespoons bacon drippings or other fat

2 cups wild lamb's-quarter, or spinach leaves and tender stems

6 green onions, sliced

8 to 10 spearmint leaves, chopped, or ½ teaspoon dried mint

Salt and pepper, to taste

Corn Griddle Cakes, page 110 (optional)

Rub grouse with 2 tablespoons of drippings. Brown on a spit over an open fire or in a skillet. Place birds and remaining ingredients in a large pot with cold water to cover. Bring to a boil. Reduce heat to low and simmer for 1½ to 2 hours, until birds are very tender. Season with salt and pepper. Serve over Corn Griddle Cakes, if desired. Serves 4 to 6

Grouse, prairie chickens, rabbits, and prairie dogs were once the first game pursued by young boys as they mastered the skills of hunting and snaring. These small seasonal game birds and animals provided welcome variety to the family diet. Young girls also contributed special treats to the cooking pot. Using skills learned from mothers and grandmothers, they gathered the greens, roots, and berries that broke the monotony of a diet consisting largely of meat.

Birds were often skinned with the feathers attached rather than plucking as we do today. This quick method allowed the whole skin with plumage to be preserved and used for decorative or ceremonial purposes.

Preheat oven to 350°F. Place cornmeal in a shallow pan and toast in oven until lightly browned, stirring frequently, about 30 minutes. While cornmeal is toasting, soak chokecherries in water to cover, then drain. Mix toasted cornmeal, chokecherries, and sugar. Add melted suet and mix thoroughly. Press the mixture into an 8-inch square pan and freeze. Cut into squares when frozen.

Makes 16 1-inch squares

SIOUX CORNMEAL PEMMICAN

(WAGMIZA WASNA)

This Sioux version of pemmican, made with parched corn instead of dried meat, is descended from a recipe of their distant agricultural past and shows the influence of farming tribes like the Hidatsa and Mandan. Corn balls made of parched ground corn and rendered fat were eaten and used by these agricultural tribes in the same way as Native Americans in other regions used meat or fish pemmican. Sometimes dried fruit and maple sugar were added to the mixture. These special corn balls were given as gifts and used as articles of trade.

In modern times, *Wagmiza Wasna* is often made with white sugar and raisins and is a candy-like treat for both adults and children.

2 cups yellow cornmeal

1 cup dried chokecherries,
   berries, or raisins
   About 1 cup water

⅓ cup sugar

1 cup melted suet or butter

Though Native American pie making on the Plains dates back only to the late 1800s, when reservations were established, the concept behind mincemeat is a very old one. Mincemeat, as we know it today, is closely related to pemmican, one of the most traditional of Native American foods. In nearly every region some version of pemmican is made. In meat-eating areas like the Plains, venison or buffalo jerky is pounded and mixed with dried berries and melted tallow. In fish-eating areas such as the Pacific Northwest, dried fish is used as the base.

Traditional pemmican is still popular Native American food but we thought that it would be interesting to show another way in which the recipe has evolved over the years. This recipe for venison mincemeat pie comes from Margaret Ketchum Walker of Cheyenne, Wyoming, whose late husband George Walker was a member of the Sac and Fox Tribe.

VENISON MINCEMEAT PIE

Mincemeat:

1 quart apple cider

2 cups seedless raisins

½ cup dried currants

½ cup dried tart or sweet cherries (If not available, currants may be substituted)

3 apples, peeled, seeded, and chopped

1 cup chopped suet

½ pound ground venison

2 teaspoons salt

2 teaspoons ground cinnamon

2 teaspoons ground ginger

2 teaspoons ground cloves

1 teaspoon grated nutmeg

½ teaspoon ground allspice

Traditional Pie Crust:

3 cups unbleached flour

1 teaspoon salt

¾ cup (12 tablespoons) lard or vegetable shortening, chilled

½ cup plus 2 tablespoons cold water

1 egg, beaten with 2 tablespoons milk or water

Make the mincemeat: In a large saucepan, combine cider, raisins, currants, and cherries. Cover and simmer over low heat for 1½ to 2 hours. Add apples, suet, venison, and spices. Simmer for 2 hours longer. If making more than a few days ahead, divide mixture in half and freeze.

Make the pie crust: In a mixing bowl, combine flour and salt. Cut in lard until mixture resembles coarse meal. Gradually stir in water until dough comes together. Turn dough onto a lightly floured surface, divide into 3 equal rounds, and wrap in waxed paper or plastic wrap. Refrigerate for at least 30 minutes before rolling out or freeze if making several days in advance. Roll out chilled rounds at least 10 inches in diameter and ¼ inch thickness. Use 2 rounds to line 9-inch pie plates. Cut remaining crust into strips for lattice tops. Chill crusts for at least ½ hour if time permits.

Preheat oven to 400°F. Fill chilled pie crusts with mincemeat. Lay lattice strips of crust over filling and brush lightly with egg wash. Fold overhanding edges of crust over strips and flute edges. Place in lower third of oven. After 15 minutes reduce oven temperature to 350°F. and bake for 40 to 50 minutes until crust is golden brown and filling is bubbling.

Makes 2 pies (12 servings)

Chokecherry pudding, sometimes called chokecherry gravy, is a popular Plains dessert that is often served with fry bread. Traditionally, when making the pudding—really a thick fruit sauce—the chokecherries are not pitted and you just spit out the seeds. Sometimes the fresh or dried chokecherries are pounded or ground, in which case the pits are eaten along with the fruit. The chokecherries are cooked with water and sweetened with honey or sugar. Originally the pudding was thickened with the parings from animal hides—though in more modern times flour, arrowroot, or cornstarch have replaced the parings.

CROW CHOKECHERRY PUDDING (BIINETTALAPPAO)

The exact method for making the pudding or gravy varies from tribe to tribe and from cook to cook. Evelyn Antelope Willow, an Arapaho cook from Wyoming who shared her chokecherry harvest with us, starts her gravy, called *re-naaku*, by combining flour and butter in a skillet to make a light brown roux. She then stirs in the chokecherries, water, and sugar, and simmers the mixture until thickened. She prefers the flavor obtained by lightly browning the flour and also tells us that many comtemporary Arapaho cooks pour their gravy through a strainer to remove the seeds.

The Crow recipe for chokecherry pudding, or *biinettalap-pao*, here was given to us by Louella Whiteman Johnson. Mrs. Johnson grew up in a Crow family with a strong sense of tradition. Her grandmother, Lizzie Yellow Tail, lived to the venerable age of one hundred and five years. "As a young girl she knew the nomadic life and yet she lived to see men walk on the moon." Mrs. Yellow Tail taught many of the old ways and customs to her children and grandchildren and the family remembers and carries on these traditions.

In a saucepan, combine chokecherries and water to cover. Cook, stirring, over medium heat until cherries soften and render their juice. Sweeten to taste. In a small bowl, combine flour and enough water to make a thin creamy mixture. Gradually stir flour into fruit mixture and simmer until thickened. Strain out the seeds, if desired. Serve alone or with Fry Bread.
Serves 4 to 6

2 cups fresh, frozen, or
   dried chokecherries
2 to 4 cups water
   Honey or sugar
¼ cup flour or 2
   tablespoons cornstarch
   or arrowroot

Mrs. Johnson, an elementary school teacher in Lodge Grass, Montana, is a great source of information about Plains cooking and native ingredients. For example, we learned that for making pudding or jelly, the Crow harvest chokecherries in early August, before they ripen fully and turn dark. "When they are bright red, the pudding has a nice tang and the jelly has a prettier color." Though traditionally they were dried for winter use, Louella now freezes fresh chokecherries and other berries and has them on hand year-round.

Similar puddings are made using serviceberries, buffalo berries, huckleberries or blueberries, wild plums, and grapes. If chokecherries are not available, you may substitute one of these other berries or fruits, though the amounts of sweetener and thickener may need to be adjusted.

Preheat oven to 375°F. In a mixing bowl, combine serviceberries, 2 tablespoons sugar, and 1 tablespoon flour.

In a separate bowl, combine remaining flour, sugar, and baking powder. Stir in water, honey, eggs, 2 tablespoons butter, vanilla, and salt to make a batter. Mix until smooth. Coat a 9-inch baking dish or ovenproof skillet with remaining butter. Spread serviceberries evenly over the bottom of the baking dish. Pour the batter over the berries. Bake for 45 to 50 minutes, until a knife inserted in the cake comes out clean. Remove from oven and carefully invert cake onto a large cake plate. Serves 6

SERVICEBERRY UPSIDE-DOWN CAKE

Serviceberries, also called sarvis berries and saskatoons, are similar to huckleberries and blueberries. These berries were a sacred food for the Cheyenne. According to modern nutritionists, they are also an excellent source of iron.

This cake recipe dates back to the early reservation period, in the late 1800s, when young girls were sent to non-Indian boarding schools and learned to bake breads and cakes.

2 cups serviceberries or blueberries

½ cup plus 2 tablespoons sugar

1½ cups unbleached flour

2 teaspoons baking powder

1 cup water

½ cup honey

2 eggs

6 tablespoons butter, melted

1 teaspoon vanilla extract

Pinch of salt

THE SOUTHWEST

THE SOUTHWEST

nique in its geography and its variety of cultures, the American Southwest includes all of New Mexico and Arizona, the southwestern corner of Colorado, and southern Utah. The region's archeological sites are remarkably preserved and the Native American cultures remain close to earlier traditions. It is home to many ethnic groups, including the Spanish and Mexican and the Anglo-American, but it is the Native Americans, who have lived here for more than 10,000 years, that fascinate us most by their spirit and enduring presence. The major groups include the Pueblo people, the Navajo, and the Pima and Papago.

The Pueblo people are village dwellers, farmers in a region of little water and minimal rainfall. Their dependence on raising corn, beans, and squash in near desert conditions led to a communal way of life and a pervasive religion linked to agriculture. Many of their daily activities, even today, focus on group ceremonies and rituals for rain and fertility.

The Navajo, originally a hunting and gathering people, developed a vigorous culture that absorbed farming and weaving skills from the Pueblo Indians, sheepherding from the Spanish, and silversmithing from the Mexicans. Over the centuries, the Navajo have shaped these elements into a way of life that is distinctly their own.

The Pima, also known as the River People, practice irrigation farming along the Gila and Salt rivers. The Papago, or Desert People, live further south in the desert where they rely on gathering mesquite beans and cactus fruit, and on practicing floodwater farming. The differences between the Pima and Papago arise from their disparate environments in central and southern Arizona, although they are essentially one people.

The Pueblo Indians of Arizona and New Mexico farm a land so arid that they must dance to attract clouds to the fields and rain from the sky. Yet their tiny corn fields, scattered about in areas where moisture accumulates, are sometimes in danger of being washed away by flash floods. Extremes of climate and the jagged contours of the land provide a setting both daunting and beautiful. Pine-spotted mesas are cut by deep canyons, and sandy washes traverse the valley floors. Summers are hot and dry, often with violent thunderstorms; winters are generally cold and snowy.

In such a world, the Pueblo people began to farm as early as two thousand years ago. They became expert at growing corn, squash, and beans in places that seemed impossible to others. Their success depended on knowledge of all growing things and on a rich and complex ceremonial cycle that, even today, binds them to Mother Earth.

At present, there are some twenty independent Pueblo villages with a total population of about 50,000. Those along the Rio Grande, including Taos, Santa Clara, San Ildefonso, San Juan, Santo Domingo, and Cochiti, comprise the Eastern Pueblos; Acoma, Zuñi, and Hopi are the major Western Pueblos. Many retain the names of saints given them by the colonizing Spanish in the late sixteenth century. Although nominally Catholic since that time, the Pueblo Indians continue their ancient native religion, which permeates every aspect of Pueblo life. Unique in its world view, it links the people with the forces of nature and with each other.

Thus the Zuñi have a creation story describing how the world—filled with life-giving plants, animals, and water—came to be. It was created in a terrace-rimmed bowl by Mother Earth. She poured water into the bowl, whipping it rapidly with her fingers. As the beaten foam rose to the rim, it covered the terraces as clouds cover the mountains. She then blew on the foam and flake after flake broke off, sending life-giving rain to fertilize the earth and nourish all that lives.

The Pueblo people today are direct descendants of the Anasazi, or Ancient Ones, dwellers in the Southwest for some 10,000 years. At first they depended on nature's yield, hunting big game and foraging for wild plants. Even now, with few rabbits and deer remaining, the Pueblo villagers continue their ancient ties with the local wild game by performing ceremonial Winter Animal Dances. Stomping and pawing the ground, their bodies swaying, long lines of men and boys dance between the village houses, wearing antlered deer headdresses and large shaggy buffalo masks. They are calling back the buffalo, deer, elk, and bighorn sheep, giving thanks to the animals who returned each season, providing sustenance that their people might live.

It was corn, however, that became vital and sacred to the Pueblos. As the climate grew warmer and drier, and herds of big game disappeared, the Anasazi turned increasingly to gathering wild fruits, nuts, berries, roots, and seeds. They developed stone implements for milling and grinding, and wove baskets of every sort—for sifting, winnowing, and storage—out of yucca and cedar fibers. Some were so tightly woven they could hold water. But nature would often withhold her bounty, and as populations increased, so did the need for a more dependable food source. Gradually, over many centuries, their intimate knowledge of native plants led to one of the world's great revolutions: corn, an agricultural miracle that evolved from a wild progenitor in Central Mexico. With great skill, the Pueblo people developed hybridized varieties, including flint, pop, dent, and sweet corn in seven colors. The Zuñi likened them to beautiful maidens: yellow as the light of winter, blue as the great world of waters, red as everlasting summer, white as the morning sky, many-colored as the clouds of evening, and black as the inside of the earth from where all emerges.

As village life became more settled, beans, a supplemental source of protein, and domesticated turkeys were introduced. Pottery was developed in many styles, without potter's wheel or kiln, but with increasing artistry, craftsmanship, and elaborate decoration. Underlying the growth and richness of Pueblo culture, however, was a widening reliance on summer rain and run-off from winter snow. Although the farmers had become ingenious in saving and diverting water, the rigors of an increasingly unstable climate and severe droughts drew them closer to supernatural spirits who could bring rain to the fields. Corn, resilient and versatile, became the major food of the Pueblos, and every ceremony called on the gods for rain, corn, and renewal.

Today, Pueblo gardens include plants that were introduced from Mexico and Europe by the Spanish—chilies, tomatoes, cabbages, apricots, peaches, and watermelons—alongside traditional foods of the Anasazi. When a Hopi farmer's corn begins to grow, he watches each plant, singing prayers of encouragement as if to a precious child. The Hopi believe corn was divinely created; a perfect ear of corn embodies the spirit of the Corn Mother, synonymous with Mother Earth, and newborn babies are blessed with ears of corn. All parts of the corn plant are used in ritual: kernels, stalks, leaves, pollen, and also cornmeal. The rising sun is greeted with cornmeal and a cornmeal path marks the road for the approaching kachinas, spirits who come down from the sacred peaks to bring rain so that all may grow. They come during cycles of planting, growth, and harvest, personated by men with painted bodies who wear ceremonial masks with feathers and evergreen boughs, foxtails, kilts, and sashes, enhanced with shell, silver, and turquoise. Their voices from within the masks, and the sound of their gourd and turtle rattles, still lead the rain to the fields under the parching sun, as they have for centuries.

The Navajo call themselves *Dineh*, the People, and their land, Navajo country, is *Dineh Bekeyah*. Here, on a reservation the size of West Virginia, they herd sheep and cattle, and farm in the legendary region of their creation. It is a vast, semi-arid land of mountains, high plains, and desert. Deep canyons cut through piñon and juniper country, extending for miles through the sage, yucca, and grasses of the tableland. Except for the sacred mountains, forested and snow-capped, the land is dry and rocky, composed of shale and petrified sand dunes.

The expansive landscape is one of incredible beauty. At times the turquoise sky is crossed by dark clouds and sudden storms that soon give way to a brief rainbow and then brilliant sun. Fantastic rock formations in glowing shades of rose and deep violet rise from the plains, and canyons of wind-gouged sandstone sweep down to the buff-colored floor below. The Painted Desert, the driest part of Navajo country, is known in Navajo as "Among the Colors."

According to the Navajo origin legend, the first *Dineh* were created by acts of the Holy People, among them First Man and First Woman, supernaturals who

Cactus Fruit Jelly

ascended through a series of lower worlds to emerge in this, the Fourth World. It was in the First World, where blue and yellow clouds met, that First Man was formed, and with him the first white corn, an ear of perfect kernels. Where yellow and blue clouds came together, First Woman was formed. With her was a perfect ear of yellow corn, white shell, and turquoise. Together with the Holy People, they struggled through each world until they reached the Fourth World. Here First Man and First Woman planned the future. They created light, the heavens, the seasons, and the first harvest. Among all of the birds and animals, it was Turkey who shook his feathered coat, dropping four kernels of corn in different colors: gray, blue, black, and red. Big Snake gave four seeds, for pumpkins, cantaloupe, watermelon, and muskmelon.

Archeological and linguistic records tell us that the Navajo were a nomadic Athabascan-speaking people who migrated into the Southwest from western Canada about 500 years ago. They were hunters, trappers, and food gatherers who moved southward in small groups, dependent upon wild plants and game animals. Those who chose the mountains as their home became the Apache. The *Dineh*, who settled near the small Pueblo villages, became the Navajo.

The Navajo hunted elk and mountain sheep in the surrounding mountains. In the lower regions, they found deer, antelope, fox, rabbit, and wild turkey. At the time of deer hunts, prayers, ceremonies, and offerings were made to ensure that these prized animals would return. But the nearby Pueblo world, settled a thousand years before the Navajo arrived, must have filled them with wonder. The Navajo saw cultivated fields of corn, beans, and pumpkins worked with stone hoes and axes. Here were decorated pottery, baskets of all sizes, and woven cotton cloth. They saw beads and ornaments made of turquoise and abalone shell being worn by the Pueblo people during their spectacular rain-bringing ceremonies. With resourcefulness and skill, the Navajo began to adapt aspects of Pueblo culture as their own, most notably corn. Although the Navajo are originally from a northern forest culture, the Navajo origin legend is centered in their new land, *Dineh Bekeyah*, with descriptions of the creation of corn and the first appearance of shell and turquoise.

Nevertheless, the Navajo did not adopt the sedentary Pueblo life. The coming of the Spanish into the Southwest, with flocks of sheep, cattle, and horses, made possible the pastoral pattern of living that has become the Navajo way. Don Juan de Oñate, the first Spanish colonizer of New Mexico, arrived in the Southwest in 1598 with the herds that were to become the Navajo's life and glory. In time, small groups of Navajo families began to build hogans in places with sufficient water for growing corn, and where they could also hunt, herd their flocks, and gather piñon. During this period, the Pueblos suffered bitterly under Spanish rule. After a century of oppression, they united to overthrow their oppressors in the Pueblo

Revolt of 1680. The Spanish fled, but many Pueblo Indians, fearful of the return of the Spanish, joined the Navajo west of the Rio Grande Valley. Here, the Pueblo people shared their knowledge and skills in agriculture and weaving, as well as the animals abandoned by the Spanish. These additional horses increased the mobility of the Navajo men, while the women and children sought pasture and water for new flocks of sheep.

By the early 1700s, the presence of Pueblo refugees had altered the Navajo diet to include not only corn, beans, and pumpkins, but chilies, watermelons, wheat, and peaches. They practiced dry farming and some irrigation, and built underground structures for the storage of food. They kept livestock, including horses, sheep, goats, and some cattle. Navajo women began wearing their own woolen cloth as they perfected the weaving skills they had learned from the Pueblo people. A visitor to a Navajo homesite in 1788 described a wide variety of foods: cooked milk, well-seasoned mutton, and many types of corn bread. Corn and wheat flour, ground by the women, was made into *atole* (a thin gruel), tortillas, piki (a paper-thin traditional Pueblo bread), and sweet bread.

The nineteenth century saw the decline of Spanish rule, a brief period of Mexican sovereignty, and a transfer of power from Mexico to the United States. It saw the Gold Rush, the completion of the transcontinental railway, and a remarkable flowering of Navajo culture. During this time, the Navajo Reservation was established, to be extended several times. The population grew so quickly that at present the *Dineh* are the largest of all American Indian tribes, numbering about 200,000. A nomadic hunting culture that arrived late in the Southwest, the Navajo have gradually altered their way of life, adapting what best suited their love of solitude, free movement, and individuality. Navajo flocks, always in need of new rangeland, have increased by the thousands. Navajo weaving is of such technical quality and stylistic originality that it admired around the world. And even today, the beloved sheep that cover the tablelands and hillsides of *Dineh Bekeyah*, along with the revered cornfields, continue to provide the staples of the Navajo diet.

The Pima and Papago are the descendants of an ancient Hohokam culture. These Indians, who live in southern Arizona near the Mexican border, first used the Salt and Gila rivers more than two thousand years ago to irrigate their fields of corn, beans, and pumpkins. The Pima maintain irrigation agriculture today, whereas the Papago are desert dwellers. In the summer, for a brief time, heavy rains flood Papago fields, but during the dry desert winter, the Papago move to camps near mountain springs where they hunt rabbit and deer.

The cultural diversity of these many tribes, stemming from historical experience and differing environments, has resulted in many delicious ways of preparing food, for sustenance, for religious observance, and for pleasure.

—Harriet Koenig

ZUÑI CORN SOUP

1 tablespoon corn oil

1 cup thinly sliced green onions

1 pound boneless venison, lamb, or goat meat, cubed

6 cups meat broth or water

4 cups fresh or frozen corn kernels

1 to 2 teaspoons ground New Mexican red chili

Salt, to taste

Fresh cilantro sprigs or chopped cilantro, for garnish

Zuñi and Hopi corn can survive in the desert-like conditions and short growing season of the high plateau of New Mexico and Arizona. It is immune to many diseases that destroy other corn and comes in a large number of desirable varieties. But the possibilities of severe drought, sand storms, flash floods, attacks by insects, and thieving birds and animals are ever-present concerns. Corn planting, therefore, is accompanied by prayers, offerings, and ceremonies to bless the endeavor and lessen the risks.

The Zuñi Corn Priest prays over the field and then sets a feathered prayer stick in its center. His prayers ask that the earth be covered with clouds to water the growing seeds. At Hopi and Zuñi pueblos, men may race across the unplanted field as they hope the rain will do, kicking a stick before them to simulate debris caught up in the torrents. To the east, among the Rio Grande pueblos, young men kick a buckskin ball full of seed corn across the field until it bursts and scatters the kernels.

Months later, after the corn is harvested, the Zuñi make a corn soup. Traditionally, it was served in a bowl set in the middle of a clean-swept, earthen-floored room for all to share.

Heat oil in a soup pot or Dutch oven. Add green onions and sauté briefly. Stir in meat and 3 cups of broth. Simmer for about 1 hour, stirring occasionally, until meat is tender. Add remaining broth, corn, chili, and salt. Simmer for about 15 minutes, until corn is tender. Serve the hot soup in bowls, topped with a cilantro sprig or chopped cilantro. Serves 4 to 6

The Anasazi cultivated squash and corn as early as the first century A.D. One early preparation for hard-shelled squash called for boiling it to a paste and mixing it with suet. This mixture was then formed into cakes and fried on hot stone slabs. Boiling whole pumpkins was another common preparation. When a boiled pumpkin was cracked open, each partaker would break off a little piece of the rind, swallow the pumpkin pulp adhering to it, and use this scoop to scrape the pulp out of the remaining pumpkin. Navajo sand paintings—used in religious ceremonies for their curative powers—often picture squash plants along with corn, beans, and tobacco.

In this soup, as in many Pueblo recipes, we see a sophisticated blend of ingredients and flavors that reflect the culinary advantages of a long-established, non-nomadic life.

PUEBLO PUMPKIN SOUP

2 tablespoons butter or vegetable oil

2 tomatoes, peeled, seeded, and chopped

1 green bell pepper, chopped

1 large onion, chopped

1 teaspoon dried mint

½ teaspoon sugar

½ teaspoon grated nutmeg

2 cups pumpkin, peeled, cubed, and cooked until tender

2 cups chicken broth

1 tablespoon unbleached flour

½ cup light cream or milk

Chopped fresh cilantro, for garnish (optional)

Melt butter in large saucepan. Add tomatoes, green pepper, onion, mint, sugar, and nutmeg, and sauté for 5 minutes. Add pumpkin and chicken broth and bring to a boil, stirring until well blended. Reduce heat to a simmer and cook, covered, for 15 to 20 minutes. Mix flour and cream until smooth and add to soup. Stir until thickened. Serve hot, garnished with chopped fresh cilantro, if desired.

Serves 4 to 6

PIÑON SOUP

Put all ingredients except garnish in large, heavy saucepan and bring to a boil. Reduce heat to a simmer and cook, covered, for 20 to 30 minutes. Puree soup in a blender or food processor until smooth. Reheat gently and serve with chopped green onions as garnish, if desired.

Note: If reheating after refrigeration, add small amount of milk or chicken broth to thin slightly.
Serves 4 to 6

Piñon pines, with their short trunks and conical tops, grow at elevations between 4,000 and 7,500 feet throughout the West. The nutritious nuts of the piñon, often called pignoli or pine nuts, are one of the oldest and most valuable food sources for Indian tribes in the region. They are a rich source of both protein and fat, containing some 3,000 calories per pound. Among the Apache, pregnant women were not allowed to eat piñons because it was thought that the nuts would increase the size of the baby and cause a difficult birth. Infants and small children, however, were often fed a gruel made from ground piñons, honey, and water.

Piñons are widely used in the baking and cooking of the Southwest. Grinding the nuts for soup is a practical and delicious way of diluting their concentrated nutritional power. This Pueblo recipe has an interesting and elegant flavor. It is rich, however, so small portions are advised.

¾ pound raw piñon nuts (pignoli)

4 cups milk

2 cups chicken broth

⅓ cup sliced green onions

2 coriander seeds, crushed

1 teaspoon dried mint, crushed

Salt and pepper, to taste

Chopped green onions, for garnish (optional)

ANASAZI BEAN SOUP

The Anasazi lived in scattered caves and rock shelters throughout the region where present-day Arizona, New Mexico, Colorado, and Utah meet. Between A.D. 400 and 700 they domesticated the tepary, or Anasazi, bean from wild varieties growing in canyons. During this same period, the Anasazi's population grew and their culture flourished. They began to make pottery, use bows and arrows, and construct multi-storied stone buildings and kivas (underground ceremonial chambers). The highly nutritious combination of beans and corn could well have provided some of the energy necessary for these cultural advances.

About four decades ago, archeologists discovered Anasazi beans among prehistoric ruins. The beans grew, and they are now sold commercially. Pueblo people, however, have cultivated these red, white, and spotted beans continuously.

1 lamb bone, cracked

1 medium onion, chopped

4 peppercorns, crushed

1 teaspoon crushed coriander seed

1 clove garlic, minced

½ teaspoon ground cinnamon

1 tablespoon thinly sliced dried red chili pods (seeds removed for a milder taste)

2 cups dried Anasazi or pinto beans, soaked overnight and drained

12 cups water

2 to 3 teaspoons salt, or to taste

Pepper, to taste

Place all ingredients except salt and pepper in a large saucepan and bring to a boil. Reduce heat to a simmer and cook, covered, for 3 to 4 hours, or until beans are tender. Remove bone from pan and shred any meat on bone. Return meat to pan and season with salt and pepper. Serve hot.
Serves 6 to 8

GARBANZO SOUP

Though they are often called beans, garbanzos (or chick-peas) are members of the pea family. Most beans are native to America, but garbanzos originated near the Mediterranean. This legume, so popular in Mediterranean countries and the Middle East, came to the American Southwest with the Conquistadors and is often an ingredient in soups and stews. The Tarahumara of southern Arizona and the Mayo of northern Mexico are its prime producers.

Salt was a rare and precious commodity in the pueblos, and Southwestern cooks learned to compensate with the skillful use of chilies and other intense flavorings. Wild onions, for example, which grow in the spring and resemble garlic, are a seasoning with authority. To distinguish them from the large, sweet Spanish onions, the Hopi and Rio Grande pueblos call them "little prairie onions"; the Zuñi name translates literally as "stinking root-nuts."

In this recipe, garlic and onion combine to mimic the flavor of their powerful wild cousin. They blend harmoniously with the heat of the chilies and provide a foil for the nutty flavor and toothsome texture of garbanzos.

Cover garbanzos with warm water and soak overnight. Drain and reserve. In a soup pot or Dutch oven, cook bacon over medium-low heat until fat is rendered. Stir in onion and garlic and cook over medium heat until translucent. Add reserved garbanzos, broth, fresh chilies, and ground chili. Over high heat, bring soup to a boil. Reduce heat to low. Cover and simmer soup for 1½ hours until garbanzos are tender. Season with salt and serve hot.
Serves 6

½ pound dried garbanzos
   (chick-peas) or 1 16-ounce
   can, drained
4 strips bacon, chopped
¼ cup chopped onion
1 clove garlic, minced
4 cups chicken broth or
   water

½ cup chopped fresh, mild,
   green chilies, peeled and
   seeded, or canned chilies
2 to 3 teaspoons medium-
   hot ground New Mexican
   red chili
   Salt, to taste

In sixteenth-century Mexico, the art of making tortillas was so important that the Franciscan missionary Fray Bernardino de Sahagún observed: "A woman who can cook has well to know how to do the following; to make good things to eat, to make tortillas, to make a good dough . . . she must know how to make her tortillas flat, and round and well formed, or on the other hand, make them long, or thin, or make them with folds." He continues: "A woman who is not good at her duties is tiresome and annoying . . . cooks tortillas badly, and her dishes are burnt or salty or sour."

Sahagún went on to describe tortillas that were white, big, and thick, made of coarsely ground flour, and thin ones made of finely ground flour from white or blue corn.

In the Pueblo villages in the more recent past, tortillas were made from a dough of finely ground corn, which was formed into balls and flattened on a smooth stone. These were laid on a very hot baking stone and constantly turned until browned on both sides. Baking stones are still in use, and some women continue to grind corn by hand, but electric grain grinders are popular. Blue corn, superior in flavor, is most often used for tortillas by Navajo and Pueblo women. If these are not available, white or yellow corn tortillas are equally good in this soup.

Heat 2 tablespoons oil in a large saucepan. Add onion and pepper and sauté until vegetables are soft. Stir in tomatoes, squash, and ground chili. Sauté for 5 minutes longer. Add broth and bring to a boil. Reduce heat to a simmer and cook, covered, for 30 minutes.

While soup is simmering, heat remaining vegetable oil in a medium skillet. Slice tortillas into ¼-inch strips. When oil is hot, but not smoking, add tortillas in several batches and fry until crisp and golden, about 10 seconds. Drain on paper towels and reserve. When soup is ready, ladle it into serving bowls and top with tortilla strips.

Serves 6

PUEBLO TORTILLA SOUP

¼ cup vegetable oil or lard

1 cup chopped onion

1 large bell pepper, chopped

¾ cup chopped tomatoes

2 cups diced summer squash or zucchini

1 to 3 teaspoons medium-hot ground New Mexican red chili

6 cups chicken broth

8 corn or flour tortillas

PUEBLO FRIED SQUASH BLOSSOMS

Squash and pumpkin blossoms are used in Indian cooking wherever these vegetables are cultivated. Only in the Southwest, however, are they important both as a cooking ingredient and as a religious symbol. The brilliant yellow-orange blossoms are used as food and as sacred symbols in Pueblo ceremonies. Representations of squash blossoms, created by winding yarns around a blossom-shaped frame, are worn by performers of Corn Dances, are used to decorate Kachina masks, and are placed on altars inside sacred ceremonial chambers called kivas.

Quantities of squash and pumpkin flowers are gathered at the end of the growing season when there is little chance that the fruits will develop. They are fried, or dried and stored in jars to be used for seasoning.

2 dozen squash blossoms
  (preferably male)
4 eggs
½ cup milk
1 teaspoon chili powder
1 teaspoon salt
¼ teaspoon ground cumin
2 to 3 cups finely ground
  cornmeal or masa harina
  Oil, for deep frying

If necessary, rinse blossoms very gently and pat dry. In a wide shallow bowl, beat eggs with milk, chili, salt, and cumin. Dip blossoms in egg mixture, then coat with cornmeal. Refrigerate for about 10 minutes to set coating. In a deep saucepan, heat 2 inches of oil until hot but not smoking, about 350°F. Fry blossoms, one or two at a time, until golden. Drain on crumpled paper towels and keep warm in oven until all have been fried. Serve immediately. Serves 4 to 6

So important are these plants that the Hopi personate them with masked dancers who embody their spirit. These kachinas, which appear during ceremonies among the Hopi and Zuñi, bring health, fertility, long life, and rain to the villages. They may be spirits of plants or animals, aspects of nature such as dawn, and even spirits of other tribes. Among the plant kachinas that dance in the Hopi village plaza is Squash Kachina or *Patung*, the Chief Kachina or *wuya* for the Pumpkin Clan. One of a group of runner kachinas, *Patung* appears in spring dances to race with men of the village, which attracts rain clouds that race across the sky to drop their moisture on dry fields of corn, beans, and squash waiting below.

This recipe calls for the larger male blossoms, but female blossoms with a tiny squash attached may also be used.

One of the many cacti that grow throughout the Southwest, the spreading prickly pear cactus has clumps of flat, oval-shaped, fleshy pods. The fruit, along the rims of the pads, sometimes called pears, have provided occasional food for many Southwestern groups. But the Pima, and especially the desert-dwelling Papago, have long depended on this cactus as a source of food. In addition to the fruit, the pads themselves, called nopales, are edible—crunchy in texture when raw because of the water they have absorbed to stave off drought.

Nopales are also eaten boiled, sometimes with garlic, onion, or even an ear of corn to sweeten them. They can be obtained, fresh or canned, at specialty food stores and in some supermarkets.

In times of drought, prickly pear pads, with the thorns singed off, are fed to livestock. The cacti themselves make very effective living fences along the borders of the cattle range. Every part of this formidable plant is put to use in the lands of the Papago, where survival is precarious.

PAPAGO CACTUS SALAD

Rinse fresh nopales well under cold running water and examine carefully to make sure all tiny thorns have been removed. Trim around the edges with scissors to remove the base of thorns. Use a sharp knife or vegetable peeler to remove a thin layer of peel. Rinse again, cut into thin strips, and simmer in lightly salted water for 5 to 6 minutes, until tender. Rinse and drain. If using canned nopales, rinse and drain well. In a salad bowl, combine lime juice, honey, chili, and oil. Add nopale strips and marinate for at least 30 minutes. Serve on a bed of greens, if desired.
Serves 4 to 6

2 to 3 5- to 7-inch fresh nopales (prickly pear cactus pads) with thorns removed or 1 7¼-ounce can natural cactus in salt water, drained

2 tablespoons lime juice, lemon juice, or vinegar

1½ teaspoons honey or sugar

½ teaspoon ground New Mexican red chili

⅓ cup sunflower or vegetable oil
Salad greens (optional)

Mash beans well and set aside. In a skillet, heat bacon drippings over medium heat. Add beans and onion and mix well. Cook, stirring occasionally, until all bacon drippings are absorbed. Season with salt. Serve with grated cheese, if desired.

Serves 4 to 6

PUEBLO REFRIED PINTO BEANS

During the short, cold days of February, the Hopi of Arizona perform *Powamu*, or the Bean Dance, to bring life and growth back to the world. *Powamu* begins in the kivas. Beans are planted in pots filled with soil and warmed by a nearby stove kept burning day and night. *Powamu* kachinas, spirits who bring rain and fertility to the villages, visit the kivas to help the sprouting beans grow. Wearing squash blossoms on their masks, they water the plants, sprinkle sacred cornmeal, and dance before them. Rapid germination and growth signal a successful planting season to come.

Of all the sacred plants, among them corn, squash, and tobacco, beans are the first to mature. In the hot, moist kivas, the dull gray drabness of winter is dispelled by the eighth day with the appearance of bright, leafy bean plants. Early that morning, the kachinas pull up the young shoots, each with a mother bean at its base, and distribute them to village households, where the Hopi women cook and serve these signs of new life to family and visitors as blessings. Some plants are saved, however, to be tied to presents for young children when they awake.

Refrying is one of many Pueblo ways of preparing beans. This dish, like tortillas, is one that many Americans think of as Mexican food. We often do not realize that these and many other Mexican dishes are in fact Indian in origin.

2 cups pinto or red kidney beans, cooked until tender, or canned
¼ cup bacon drippings
1 tablespoons finely chopped onion
Salt, to taste
Grated cheese (optional)

2 to 3 5- to 7-inch fresh nopales (prickly pear cactus pads) with thorns removed or 1 7¼-ounce can natural cactus in salt water, drained

Salt

4 strips bacon, diced

½ cup chopped onion

½ to 1 teaspoon ground New Mexican red chili or chili powder

4 to 6 eggs

Ground pepper (optional)

PIMA-PAPAGO CACTUS AND EGGS

Cactus serves as food in the hottest and driest regions of the Southwest, where annual rainfall can average as little as five inches in some areas. Here, the Pima depend on irrigation from the Gila and Salt rivers for their crops, but often water is scarce. The Papago reservation has neither rivers nor permanent streams, so Papago farming is less intensive and the Papago rely on hunting and gathering. The many types of cacti can be counted on, regardless of the vagaries of rainfall, and are part of the diet and the ritual life of these two tribes.

In a place that is bone dry, the barrel cactus—with deep ridges and large black thorns—furnishes a quantity of whitish liquid when crushed on top with a stone. A cup or gourd, pushed down inside, soon fills with a good substitute for water.

The cholla cactus is covered with thorns that seem to reach out and catch anything that comes near. Also known as "jumping cactus," the cholla is used by medicine men to dispel illness. Using a branch of cholla, they wave the cactus over the patient with chants and prayers so the illness will be caught up and stick to the thorns.

This recipe, which uses the pads of the prickly pear cactus, is particularly good served with Sacaton Relish or salsa and tortillas or bread.

Rinse fresh nopales well under cold running water and examine carefully to make sure all tiny thorns have been removed. Trim around the edges with scissors to remove the base of thorns. Use a sharp knife or vegetable peeler to remove a thin layer of peel. Rinse again, cut into thin strips, and simmer in lightly salted water for 5 to 6 minutes, until tender. Rinse and drain. If using canned nopales, rinse and drain.

Cook bacon until crisp in a large skillet over medium-low heat. Remove with a slotted spoon and reserve.

Add onion and chili to the drippings in skillet. Sauté over medium heat until onion is translucent. Stir in reserved cactus strips and bacon. Sauté briefly. Break desired number of eggs on top of cactus mixture. Cover tightly and cook over low heat for 5 to 7 minutes, until whites are set and yolks are cooked to taste. Sprinkle lightly with salt and pepper, if desired.

Serves 4 to 6

Sacaton is a village on the Pima reservation. The relish recipe that follows is typical of the cooked salsas made in that region. It is usually served as an accompaniment to eggs or grilled meat, and is especially good with Pima-Papago Cactus and Eggs.

SACATON RELISH

Heat drippings in a skillet. Add chilies and jalapeño and sauté over medium heat until tender. Stir in onion and sauté until translucent. Add tomatoes and sauté 5 minutes more. Season with salt, if desired. Remove relish with a slotted spoon and serve with eggs or meat.
Makes approximately 1½ cups relish

2 tablespoons bacon
   drippings or vegetable oil
1 cup chopped fresh, mild,
   green chilies, peeled and
   seeded
1 chopped fresh or canned
   jalapeño
½ cup chopped onion
3 medium tomatoes,
   seeded and diced
   Salt (optional)

Pat meat dry so it will brown properly. Heat the oil in a large deep skillet over medium-high heat. Add meat, onion, and chili and sauté until meat is lightly browned and onion is softened. Stir in tomatoes, corn, and beans and reduce the heat to low. Simmer for about 15 minutes, until meat is cooked and vegetables are tender. Stir in crushed sunflower seeds and season with salt and pepper. Simmer for another 15 to 20 minutes, until succotash has thickened.

Serves 4 to 6

1 pound uncooked venison or beef, cut into small pieces

2 tablespoons corn oil or bacon drippings

1 cup chopped onion

1 to 2 teaspoons ground New Mexican red chili or 1 tablespoon chili powder

2 cups peeled, seeded, and diced tomatoes

2 cups fresh or frozen corn kernels

2 cups fresh or frozen green beans, cut into 2-inch lengths

2 tablespoons hulled sunflower seeds, crushed Salt and pepper, to taste

ZUÑI SUCCOTASH

The word "succotash" comes from the Northeastern Narraganset Indian word "Msickquatash," which means "a whole ear of corn." But this famed dish is also very popular among the Zuñi, who prepare it with green corn, the young sweet ears that are available only in early summer.

One December, we watched the Zuñi *Shalako* ceremony, when the messengers of the rain gods come to the Zuñi villages. They danced—tall, wingless birds with huge beaks and popping eyes—to bless the new houses. The ceremony continued until dawn, and the many guests who followed the *Shalako* from house to house in the snowy evening became cold and hungry. While the dancing was taking place in the main room of the new house, the crowd was fed in the side rooms by patient women with platters of mutton stew, roasted chicken, bread, strong coffee, and Zuñi succotash, which was made with dried corn as suited the winter season.

NAVAJO FRY BREAD

Fry bread is one of the most widespread of modern Indian foods. It is served at powwows, rendezvous, and other Native American gatherings in all regions as a festive snack and is also part of everyday cooking. Though the recipe varies slightly from one tribe and one cook to another, the basic ingredients—flour, baking powder, salt, and water or milk—remain the same. The basic dough is patted or rolled into the desired shape—round, square, or triangular, depending on the region—and deep-fried until puffed, crisp, and golden.

Fry bread is often served with honey or powdered sugar. Among the Plains tribes a sweetened chokecherry gravy or sauce is popular.

In a mixing bowl, combine all ingredients except oil and knead until smooth. Rub oil or shortening over dough. Cover and let sit for about 30 minutes. Either pat or roll out enough dough to fit in the palm of your hand in a circle about ⅛ inch thick, and deep-fry in hot oil or shortening. Usually the Fry Bread is a little larger than the size of your hand.
Makes 10 to 12 Fry Breads

3 cups unbleached flour
2 teaspoons baking
powder (increase to
3 teaspoons at high
altitudes)
1 teaspoon salt
1½ cups warm water or
milk
1 tablespoon oil or
shortening
Oil or shortening, for
deep frying

There are also savory versions of fry bread. We have tasted a Southwestern rendition with chopped onions and chilies mixed into the dough. Another great favorite in that region is the Indian taco. Fry bread is topped with traditional taco ingredients such as ground beef, lettuce, tomato, cheese, and salsa. It is messy, but delicious, if eaten hot.

This basic recipe for fry bread comes from Helen Begay, a Navajo of the *Naakai Dinee* or "Mexican" Clan (maternal) and the *Ashiihi* or "Salt" Clan (paternal). Mrs. Begay was born at Lukachukai in the heart of the Navajo reservation and now lives in Los Alamos, New Mexico. Since the altitude there is 7,000 feet, she uses 3 teaspoons of baking powder in this recipe; 2 teaspoons will suffice at lower altitudes.

UTE TORTILLAS

Helen Begay suggested that we include this alternate cooking method for fry bread dough, which comes from the Ute tribe, the Navajos' neighbor to the north.

Made with the same dough as Fry Bread, Ute Tortillas are formed in the same way as fry bread but cooked over charcoal outdoors on a grill or over an open fire. "This tastes very different. It is served with roasted meat, fried potatoes, and green chilies," Helen told us. We tried it and found it to be delicious.

Opposite: Fry Breads and Indian Tacos

6 strips lean bacon

2 cups yellow, blue, or
white cornmeal

1 tablespoon sugar

2 teaspoons salt

2 teaspoons baking soda

1 teaspoon ground
New Mexican red chili
or chili powder

1¼ cups buttermilk

2 eggs

¼ cup chopped green
onions

¼ cup chopped mild green
chilies

1 seeded and chopped
fresh or canned jalapeño
(optional)

The Zuñi kitchen of one hundred years ago had cooking utensils hanging from the rafters and walls—sieves of coarsely woven yucca, trays for cornmeal, and wicker bread plaques. On the floor were large cooking pots, stone-lidded water containers, polished baking stones, bread bowls to hold the rising dough, hardwood pokers, pudding sticks, and bundles of finely splintered piñon wood. The fireplace extended across one side of the room. In a corner of the fireplace, a large, thick baking stone sat on four short masonry supports. At the opposite corner were supports for heavy cooking pots. In the middle of the fireplace, an oven-like stone cist was sunk deep into the ground.

Although the fireplace remains today, modern Pueblo kitchens more often depend on gas stoves. Skillet corn bread, popular with both Pueblo and Navajo cooks, is often cooked on top of the stove, but can as easily be cooked outdoors on an improvised campfire stove.

SKILLET CORN BREAD

In an 8- to 9-inch heavy iron skillet, cook bacon until crisp over medium-low heat. Remove bacon, drain on paper towels, crumble, and reserve. Reserve drippings in skillet.

Preheat oven to 350°F. In a large mixing bowl, sift together cornmeal, sugar, salt, and baking soda. In a separate bowl, beat together 1 tablespoon of reserved drippings, chili powder, buttermilk, and eggs.

Heat skillet over medium heat, turning to coat well with remaining drippings. Stir wet ingredients into the dry ones and fold in bacon, green onions, chilies, and jalapeño. Pour batter into the preheated skillet and bake for about 30 minutes, until a knife inserted in the center of the bread comes out clean and the top is golden brown. Cut in wedges and serve directly from the skillet.

Note: To make this corn bread on top of a stove, cover the skillet and cook over low heat for about 15 minutes. Invert the bread onto the lid or a plate and slide back into the skillet. Cook, covered, for another 10 to 15 minutes, until a knife inserted in the center of the bread comes out clean. This method works very well and is a good one to remember when camping or anytime you don't have an oven available, but the oven baking method is a bit easier, as no inverting is required and browning tends to be more even.
Serves 4 to 6

NAVAJO KNEEL DOWN BREAD

There are many variations in Native American cooking on the idea of a soft "bread" made from ground or pureed fresh corn that is wrapped in fresh or dried corn husks and boiled, steamed, or baked in a pit dug under the cooking fire. Kneel Down Bread is the Navajo version of this dish. According to legend, its name comes from its traditional cooking method: the bread was baked in a pit and the cook was obliged to kneel down to tend to the cooking.

This recipe is an interesting variation on plain Kneel Down Bread. Marilyn Yazzie, a Navajo from Ganado, Arizona, supplied the recipe. Marilyn recalls that her grandmother also sometimes made a sweet version of Kneel Down Bread by adding pureed peaches, apples, or prickly pear pulp to the corn.

5 ears fresh corn

1 12-ounce can corned beef

½ cup chopped fresh green chilies, peeled and seeded, or 1 4-ounce can

1 egg, lightly beaten
   Corn husks, soaked in water

Scrape corn from cob into a mixing bowl. Mash corn to a pulp. Add corned beef, chilies, and egg. Mix well. Pat husks dry and lay out, with overlapping edges, to form a 7 × 12-inch rectangle. Place corn mixture in the middle of the rectangle and form into a loaf. Fold husks over loaf and tie with string or wrap in aluminum foil. Place on a baking sheet and bake in a preheated 350°F. oven for 60 to 75 minutes, until loaf is cooked through and set. Unwrap, slice, and serve.
Serves 4 to 6

1 cup blue cornmeal

1 tablespoon sugar

2 teaspoons baking powder

1 teaspoon baking soda

1 teaspoon salt

3 tablespoons melted butter
   or shortening

2 eggs, beaten

1 cup milk
   Butter and honey or
   syrup, for serving

Corn has a long history: In 1954, fossil pollen grains found in Mexico City in a drill core from a depth of 200 feet were dated to about 80,000 B.C., long before human beings are believed to have reached this continent. Ten years later, the archeologist R. S. MacNeish found prehistoric wild corn that dated from around 5,000 B.C. in a once-inhabited cave in the Tehuacan Valley in southern Mexico.

Blue corn has long been favored in the Southwest, and it has been suggested that it may surpass other varieties in food value. This could well be a side effect of the method of preparation, in which the ashes of juniper and salt bush are mixed with the cornmeal to maintain its blue color. This alkali treatment releases more nutrients.

Traditionally, the griddle used for cooking the cakes in this recipe would be made of very smooth sandstone, but a modern metal griddle or frying pan will work just as well. Helen Begay, a Navajo, tells us that her family used goat's milk in the griddle cake batter and that "the milk was so sweet that we could eat our cakes without syrup."

PUEBLO BLUE CORN GRIDDLE CAKES

Combine dry ingredients in a mixing bowl. Stir in butter, eggs, and milk, and mix well. Allow batter to rest for 10 minutes before cooking. Drop batter by tablespoonfuls onto a medium-hot, lightly greased griddle. When bubbles form on top, after about 2 minutes, turn cakes and cook until they are lightly browned on the other side. Serve with butter and honey or syrup.

Makes about 12 3-inch cakes

Place flour in a mixing bowl. Slowly add water and stir constantly to make a thick batter. Stir in egg, baking powder, chilies, and onion. Mix well.

Heat oil to 360°F., or until a cube of bread dropped in oil browns in 30 seconds. Drop batter by tablespoonfuls into hot oil and fry until golden brown. Remove with a slotted spoon and drain on paper towels. Serve immediately.

Makes 10 fritters

PUEBLO CHILI FRITTERS

⅔ cup unbleached flour

⅓ cup water

1 egg, lightly beaten

½ teaspoon baking powder

½ cup mild (or combined mild and hot) fresh green chilies, roasted, peeled, seeded, and chopped, or

1 4-ounce can

2 tablespoons minced onion

Oil, for deep frying

"Chili" is the Aztec word for a plant used by the Maya of Yucatan a millennium earlier. As its fame spread to distant parts of the New World, it became a basic condiment in American Indian cooking, relished in its fresh, green form, or enjoyed dried, after turning red. Among the fresh chilies are the bright green and smooth-skinned jalapeños and the long, triangular, dark green poblanos. The "Chimayo" chili, named for a local village, is grown in the Espanola Valley of New Mexico, north of Santa Fe, by descendants of the early Spanish settlers. When grown in California, the "Chimayo" pepper—called the "Anaheim" or "California"—lacks the special flavor that the New Mexican environment produces.

After harvesttime, double strings of chilies turn deep shades of red as they hang from roof beams, drying in the autumn sun. The urge to photograph these brilliant "chiles de ristra" against sand-colored adobe walls and a cloudless blue sky is almost irresistible.

Fritters are popular in Indian cooking throughout the country. Originally they were fried in bear grease or lard, but you can use oil or shortening.

1 ¼-ounce package active dry yeast

½ cup lukewarm water

1½ cups hot water

2 tablespoons lard or vegetable shortening

1 tablespoon sugar

1 teaspoon salt

4½ to 5½ cups unbleached flour

PUEBLO ADOBE BREAD

A visitor to any pueblo may notice large, dome-shaped structures—four feet high or more—placed among the Pueblo dwellings. Called beehive ovens, or *hornos* in Spanish, they resemble ovens used in Spain hundreds of years ago. Each oven is constructed of stones and plastered with adobe, a mixture of clay, sand, and straw that dries as hard as stucco. Before baking, a fire inside the oven is allowed to burn out and the ashes are swept away. Then, using wooden shovels, loaves of bread or other foods are put in to bake. A sheet of galvanized iron usually covers the square oven door. During summer Corn Dances, booths are set up in the plaza, where native foods are sold next to modern snacks. But most popular among visitors are the crusty, golden, round loaves of adobe bread sold by the Pueblo women who baked them that morning.

Preheat oven to 375°F. In a small bowl, dissolve yeast in lukewarm water and set aside. In a large mixing bowl, combine hot water, lard, sugar, and salt. Add 1 cup flour and beat well. Stir in yeast until thoroughly combined. Add 3 to 3½ cups flour, beating thoroughly. Turn onto a lightly floured surface and knead for 10 minutes, adding more flour, if necessary, until dough is smooth and elastic. Place dough in a greased bowl, cover with a towel, and let rise in a warm place until doubled in bulk, about 1 hour. Punch down and divide dough in half. Place in 2 smaller greased ovenproof bowls, turning once so the tops are greased, and bake for 45 to 50 minutes, or until tops are nicely browned. Turn loaves out and let cool on a rack.

Makes 2 loaves or 12 servings

Preheat oven to 350° F. In a mixing bowl combine flour, pumpkin, sugar, butter, eggs, baking powder, cinnamon, nutmeg, and salt. Stir in piñon nuts. Place batter in a greased 6×9-inch bread pan. Bake for 1 hour, or until a knife inserted in bread comes out clean.

Serves 6 to 8

PUEBLO PUMPKIN-PIÑON BREAD

1½ cups unbleached flour

1 cup mashed or pureed cooked pumpkin

¾ cup sugar

½ cup butter, melted

2 eggs, beaten

1 teaspoon baking powder

1 teaspoon ground cinnamon

1 teaspoon grated nutmeg

½ teaspoon salt

¾ cup shelled piñon nuts (pignoli)

Spaniards arriving in New Mexico in the late fifteenth century found the Pueblo people along the Rio Grande growing many kinds of squash, including pumpkins, which continue to be an important ingredient in the cooking of all of the major tribes of this region. The pumpkin is valued for its flesh and seeds, and makes a handy edible cooking pot for soups and stews.

There are few kinds of nuts available in the Southwest, but piñon nuts—found in the cones of the pinon pine, a dwarf tree that covers the rocky hills of New Mexico and Arizona—provide delicious compensation. About twice the size of rice grains, they grow within tightly closed pine cones. In September, the cones open and the piñons fall to the ground. Pueblo and Navajo families go out to gather these fallen seeds, some camping for many weeks until the snow comes. The nuts are freed from the particles of earth and pine needles by winnowing, or straining out the impurities. Winnowing baskets are partly filled, held high, shaken to the wind, and tipped so that only the nuts remain. Strainers made by stretching wire mesh across a square wooden frame accomplish the same purpose, although with less grace.

In the Pueblo recipe below, these two traditional ingredients are combined in a spicy, cake-like bread. Serve it lightly toasted as a sweet bread or at room temperature for dessert.

Piñon nuts—which, like acorns and sunflower seeds, are rich in protein—have long been an important part of the Southwestern diet. Piñons are sometimes eaten raw, but are best when roasted over a fire in a large bowl, in which they are constantly stirred so they will not burn. Before the invention of pottery, the Zuñi parched piñons in shallow basket trays plastered with clay. They combined a few glowing coals with two or three quarts of nuts, and shook the basket using a spiral motion to keep the contents dancing about. The nuts browned evenly while the basket was protected by the thin coating of clay. This clay became a hardened replica of the basket and gave rise to the idea of pottery. Roasted piñons were reheated and rolled lightly under a grinding stone to break their brittle skins and release the sweet, oily nut meats.

Because of their high fat content, piñons cannot be reduced to ground meal. Rather, a paste can be made by roasting the nut meats again and then lightly grinding them on a fine-grained stone. The Zuñi formed the paste into small cakes, wrapped them in leaves, and stored them, buried in ashes. Because of their high nutritional content and delicious taste, piñon cakes were used as a meat substitute. This recipe is for a modern version.

PIÑON CAKES

1½ cups whole wheat flour

2 teaspoons baking powder

¾ teaspoon salt

½ cup piñon nuts (pignoli), ground to fine meal

2 tablespoons sugar

2 tablespoons butter, margarine, or lard, chilled

½ cup water

Sift flour, baking powder, and salt into a mixing bowl. Stir in ground nuts and sugar. Add butter in small bits, combining with fingers until mealy. Add water gradually until a medium-soft dough is formed. Knead for 5 minutes and place in a greased bowl. Cover and let rest for 15 minutes. Pinch off egg-sized balls of dough and roll with a rolling pin to a ⅛-inch thickness. Place on a lightly greased griddle and cook about 3 minutes on each side, until golden. Serve these crisp cakes warm topped with honey and butter, or at room temperature in place of crackers.
Makes 10 cakes

**1 ¼-ounce package active
 dry yeast**
¼ cup lukewarm water
3½ cups unbleached flour
**2 teaspoons crushed dried
 sage**
1 tablespoon sugar
1 teaspoon salt
¼ teaspoon baking soda
1 egg
1 cup cottage cheese
**1 tablespoon melted
 vegetable shortening or
 lard**

Breads and porridges made of cornmeal or wheat flour are a staple of the Navajo diet. For the early Navajo, mush was particularly convenient to prepare. Cornmeal, stirred with boiling water or goat's milk with a pinch of cedar ashes, yielded a dish the consistency of mashed potatoes that could be eaten when cool. The mush could also be wrapped in corn husks and covered with hot embers to bake. Sometimes unbaked mush was saliva-sweetened and allowed to freeze overnight, to be enjoyed as a kind of winter ice cream.

Later, wheat—either ground on the *metate* or as flour bought at the trading post—was used in addition to cornmeal by Navajo cooks. Various breads are still baked in small, underground pit ovens, first heated and then lined with corn husks. The dough is poured in, covered with a second layer of corn husks and then a light layer of earth, over which a fire is kept burning throughout the night. Loaves, or sometimes biscuits, can also be baked in the hot embers.

Among the many plants Navajo cooks use as seasonings, wild sage has a place in curing ceremonies as well. Helen Begay.recalls gathering this herb as a child for her mother's kitchen in Lukachukai on the Navajo reservation. Wild sage is also placed on the heated sand floor of the sudatory, or sweat-bath house, during curing rituals, because its pleasant, pungent odor attracts good.

In discussing this recipe, Helen recalled that her mother made a fresh cheese from goat's milk that resembled present-day cottage cheese.

NAVAJO WILD SAGE BREAD

Dissolve yeast in lukewarm water and set aside. Combine dry ingredients in a mixing bowl. In a large mixing bowl, beat egg and cottage cheese until smooth. Stir in melted shortening and yeast. Add flour mixture gradually, beating vigorously after each addition, until a stiff dough is formed. Place dough on a lightly floured surface and knead for 10 minutes. Cover dough with a cloth and let rise in a warm, draft-free place for 1 to 1½ hours, or until it doubles in bulk. During the last period of rising, preheat the oven to 375°F. Punch down dough and knead for 1 minute.

Place dough in a greased, 2-quart ovenproof bowl and bake for 50 minutes, until it is golden brown and firm to the touch. Turn bread out of its bowl and cool on a rack. Serves 6 to 8

The Hopi are sometimes called "the people of the blue corn." Their creation legend tells how they chose this corn above all others because although it was small, it would endure. The Hopi cultivate corn of all colors in valley plots far from their mesa-top dwellings, but they favor the stubby blue ears. Corn grinding was described by Pedro de Castañeda in his letters to Spain during the Coronado Southwest Expedition of 1540–1542:

> They keep the separate houses where . . . they grind the meal very clean . . . They have a trough with three stones fixed in stiff clay. Three women go in here, each one having a stone, with which one of them breaks the corn, the next grinds it, and the third grinds it again. . . . A man sits at the door, playing on a fife, while they grind, moving the stones to the music and singing together. They grind a large quantity at one time because they make all their bread of meal soaked in warm water, like wafers.

This recipe uses both fresh corn kernels and blue cornmeal. Pueblo visitors today, seeing huge stacks of blue corn, may wonder how Hopi women manage all the grinding—until they see a truck arrive with a motorized grinding machine, which can process hundreds of pounds at a time.

At Zuñi, the inhabitants make dumplings using blue cornmeal mixed with yeast and formed into pellets, then wrapped tightly in corn shucks. When boiled, these dumplings become very blue as they swell up from the yeast.

HOPI CORN STEW
WITH BLUE DUMPLINGS

2 tablespoons bacon drippings or oil
1½ pounds ground beef or goat meat
1 medium onion, chopped
1 large green bell pepper, seeded and chopped
1 tablespoon ground New Mexican red chili
4 cups fresh or frozen corn kernels
1 small zucchini
1 small yellow squash or 2 cups diced pumpkin
4 to 5 cups water
2 tablespoons whole wheat flour
Salt, to taste
Blue Dumplings

Heat oil over medium-high heat in a large stew pot or Dutch oven. Add meat and sauté until lightly browned. Stir in onion, pepper, and ground chili. Sauté until onion is translucent, 3 to 4 minutes. Stir in corn, zucchini, and squash and add enough water to cover. Bring to a boil, then reduce heat to medium-low and simmer for 30 to 40 minutes, until meat and vegetables are tender.

In a small bowl combine the flour and 2 tablespoons of broth from the stew. Whisk back into the stew and simmer until thickened. Add Blue Dumplings to the simmering stew during the last 15 minutes of cooking time.

Serves 6

BLUE DUMPLINGS

2 cups blue cornmeal
2 teaspoons baking powder
2 tablespoons bacon drippings
½ teaspoon salt
⅔ to 1 cup milk

In a mixing bowl combine cornmeal, baking powder, bacon drippings, and salt. Stir in enough milk to make a stiff batter. Drop by tablespoonfuls into the stew during last 15 minutes of cooking time.

PUEBLO CARROT HASH

Pueblo gardeners have grown carrots for many years, but wild carrots grew and were gathered and eaten by Native Americans in many parts of the country long before carrots became a cultivated crop. This Pueblo preparation of carrots is unusual and delicious.

2 pounds carrots
½ cup butter or margarine
1 tablespoon dark brown
   sugar
½ cup orange juice
   Salt, to taste

Wash and grate carrots. Melt butter in a large skillet and add carrots and sugar. Cover and cook over medium heat for 10 minutes, stirring several times. Add orange juice and cook 5 minutes more, uncovered, until carrots are cooked but crunchy. Season with salt.
Serves 4 to 6

Heat oil in large heavy skillet. Add lamb and sauté over medium-high heat until lightly browned, 5 to 8 minutes. (Brown in 2 batches if necessary to avoid crowding.) Remove lamb and reserve. Add onion and garlic and cook over medium heat until onion is translucent, 5 to 6 minutes. Return meat to pan and add remaining ingredients. Simmer over medium-low heat for about 2 hours, until meat is tender. Add dumplings and simmer 20 minutes longer.

¼ cup vegetable oil

2 pounds boneless lamb, cut into cubes

1 large onion, chopped

2 cloves garlic, minced

3 tablespoons chili powder (if using New Mexican red, season to taste) Salt and ground pepper, to taste

3 large tomatoes, peeled, seeded, and coarsely chopped

2 cups cooked pinto or black beans

2 potatoes, peeled and diced

3 cups lamb broth or water Corn Dumplings

The Pueblo people have separate rituals for foods from animals and corn, but the Navajo combine them in their mythology. Sacred stories tell of animals that hunt, carrying packs of corn on their backs, and of game animals—such as mountain sheep—that carry seeds of all plants. The Plume Way Chant stresses the advantages of a diet of both meat and vegetables.

After the Navajo settled among Pueblo farmers, they adopted Pueblo colored corn, emphasizing its preciousness by associating it with their four sacred mountains: white for east, blue for south, yellow or red for west, and black for north.

The Navajo sing many farm songs during the planting and maturation of corn. From the time the seeds are put into the ground until the harvest, they sing of sprouting, of the first tiny blades that appear above ground, of the yellow-green color of the fields, of the growth of leaves that touch when the wind blows, and of the appearance of corn silk and pollen. Songs sung at harvest describe the stacking of ears of corn and the crackling sound of the dry stalks.

NAVAJO LAMB STEW

WITH CORN DUMPLINGS

CORN DUMPLINGS

2 cups corn kernels

1 cup unbleached flour

3 tablespoons cornmeal

2 teaspoons baking powder

1 teaspoon salt

4 tablespoons butter, softened

1 to 2 tablespoons milk

Place corn in a mixing bowl and mash with a fork. Stir in flour, cornmeal, baking powder, and salt. Cut in butter. Add enough milk to form a stiff batter. Drop mixture by tablespoonfuls into the stew. Serves 6

Rinse posole in cold water until water runs clear. Soak it for several hours in cold water. Place posole with water to cover in a large pot or Dutch oven. Bring to a boil over medium-high heat. Reduce heat to low and simmer, covered, until posole pops, about 1 hour. Add chilies, jalapeños, onion, garlic, tomato, and pork. Simmer, covered, about 4 hours until meat is tender. Shred meat and return it to the pot. Season with oregano and salt. Simmer, covered, for at least 1 additional hour.

Note: Frozen or canned posole is also available in some areas and may be substituted. If using either of these products, soaking is not necessary and cooking time may be reduced by about 1 hour.
Serves 4 to 6

2 cups blue posole (dried whole hominy)

½ cup mild fresh green chilies, roasted, peeled, and chopped, or 1 4-ounce can

1 to 3 fresh or canned jalapeños, peeled, seeded and chopped

½ cup chopped onion

2 cloves garlic, minced

1 peeled, seeded, and chopped tomato (about ¾ cup)

2- to 3-pound boneless pork roast

2 teaspoons dried Mexican oregano (optional)

Salt, to taste

NAVAJO POSOLE

Many Indian tribes made hominy from their corn in a traditional manner by cooking it in a mixture of wood or corn-cob ashes, powdered lime, and water, which removed the tough outer covering of the kernels. The term "posole" is used to describe both the major ingredient of this recipe—whole hominy—and the dish itself, a hearty stew. Posole, one of the most popular Southwestern Indian recipes, is often served at feasts during the Christmas and New Year's season in Indian, Mexican, and Anglo homes throughout New Mexico and Arizona. Hominy made from blue corn is preferred, but white and yellow varieties are also used.

This Posole recipe was given to us by Marilyn Yazzie, a Navajo of the *Tsenjikini*, or "Honey Combed Rock" Clan (maternal), and the *Tachiinnii*, or "Red Running into the Water" Clan (paternal), who works at the Hubbell Trading Post in Ganado, Arizona. She favors fresh green rather than dried red chilies in Posole, and likes it hot. For a milder taste, use only one jalapeño or add more mild green chili and eliminate the jalapeño entirely. A health-conscious cook, Marilyn chooses lean cuts of pork and adds no salt to her Posole.

Game was hunted in the Southwest before the arrival of white settlers, first the Spanish, then the Americans. Hopi and other Pueblo men pursued deer, antelope, mountain sheep, mountain lion, fox, and badger. All parts of the animals were used: skins for clothing, sinew for sewing and fastenings, bone for tools, hoofs for ceremonial rattles, and meat for eating.

With the ever-increasing incursion of livestock, pasture-land and wooded areas began to disappear from overuse. Game became scarce, the Pueblo diet became largely vege-tarian, and meat was reserved for special occasions. Killed animals brought back from the hunt were decorated with blankets and turquoise and treated with respect to appease their spirits in the hope that they would return.

Deer, antelope, and mountain sheep—seldom found in the region today—remain alive in the winter animal dances of many Pueblo tribes. In these ceremonies, the costumed dancers wear antlers, animal skins, and heavy circles of evergreen branches around their necks, re-creating the animals amid their forest environment.

HOPI VENISON STEW

2 pounds venison, cut into 1½-inch cubes
½ cup unbleached flour
¼ cup vegetable oil
1 medium onion, chopped
1 cup diced celery
¼ cup hot or mild fresh green chilies or a combination of the two, peeled, seeded, and diced, or ½ 4-ounce can
4 cups water
1 tablespoon dried Mexican oregano
1½ cups sliced carrots
2 potatoes, peeled and cut into ½-inch cubes
1 cup diced yellow turnip (rutabaga)

Pat venison dry with a clean towel and dredge lightly in flour. Heat oil in a large skillet and brown the meat well on all sides. Transfer meat to a stew pot or Dutch oven. In the same oil, sauté onion, celery, and chilies until onion is translucent. Add vegetables to the pot along with water and oregano. Bring stew to a boil. Reduce heat to low, cover, and simmer for 1½ to 2 hours, until meat is almost tender. Add carrots, potatoes, and turnips. Cook an additional 20 to 30 minutes, until potatoes are tender.
Serves 6

Pat beef dry with a clean towel. Flour meat lightly and reserve. In a large, ovenproof saucepan or Dutch oven, cook onion, bacon, and garlic over medium heat for 3 to 4 minutes. Remove to a separate dish and reserve. Add oil to the saucepan and brown meat on all sides.

Return bacon, onion, and garlic to the pan and stir in tomatoes, broth, chilies, jalapeños, cumin, oregano, and salt and pepper to taste. Simmer, covered, over low heat for 1½ hours. Add garbanzos and continue to simmer for an additional hour, or until meat and vegetables are tender.

Serves 6

PUEBLO BEEF STEW WITH

GREEN CHILIES AND GARBANZOS

It is estimated that agricultural foods had increased to about 80 percent of the Pueblo diet at the time of first contact with Europeans. Limited quantities of meat came from hunting game and rabbits. Buffalo meat, obtained in trade with the Plains Indians, entered the Pueblo diet after the Spanish brought horses to the Plains tribes. One of these tribes, the Comanche, desired Pueblo agricultural products and came to trade. As described in 1890 by the explorer Adolph Bandelier, the Comanche obtained cornmeal, bread, dried apples, melons, pottery, turquoise, and cotton blankets. In exchange the Pueblo traders received unique bows made of Osage orange wood, occasionally horses, and dried buffalo meat, hides, and buffalo heads used for ritual purposes.

After cattle were brought to the Southwest and the buffalo had disappeared, beef gradually replaced buffalo meat in the Pueblo diet. During a visit to the home of the famed potter Margaret Gutierrez on the feast day of Santa Clara Pueblo, a pot of meat stew bubbled on the stove. When asked whether it was beef or lamb, Margaret laughed and said, "Why it's buffalo, of course. This is an Indian feast." Later she told us it was really beef, although buffalo would have revived happy memories of the past.

2 pounds top round stewing beef
½ cup unbleached flour
2 cups chopped onion
4 slices bacon, chopped
2 cloves garlic, minced
3 to 4 tablespoons vegetable oil
2 large tomatoes, peeled, seeded, and chopped
2 cups beef broth or water
2 cups chopped mild, fresh green chilies, peeled and seeded, or 4 4-ounce cans
1 to 2 minced fresh or canned jalapeños (optional)
1 teaspoon ground cumin
½ teaspoon dried Mexican oregano
Salt and ground pepper, to taste
1½ cups dried garbanzos (chick-peas), soaked overnight, or 1 16-ounce can

NAVAJO STUFFED SWEET PEPPERS

**2 tablespoons butter or
vegetable oil**

**1 pound lamb, cut into ½-
inch pieces**

**1½ cups chopped fresh
tomatoes or canned
tomatoes, drained**

**1 cup unseasoned white
bread crumbs**

¼ cup chopped onion

**½ teaspoon ground
coriander seed**

**½ teaspoon ground cumin
Salt and pepper, to taste**

4 large sweet bell peppers

**1 tablespoon chopped
fresh cilantro, if desired,
for garnish**

From the time the Navajo first acquired sheep, their flocks have been central to Dineh culture. Herding is a daily activity throughout the year, setting up a pattern of movement to areas that afford the best grass and water. All family members are experienced herders, but traditionally, most herding was done by children. They stayed with the flocks—goats and sheep together—spreading them over a pasture, guarding against coyotes, and listening for the bells on older animals that helped locate the flocks as they moved. In his autobiography, *Son of Old Man Hat*, Left Handed describes his childhood among the sheep: ". . . I began to herd around the hogan, in the morning and evening when the sheep came home. But I was so small, I went out with the sheep like a dog. I just walked along with them and stayed right in the middle of the herd. I was afraid to go around them, but while I was in the middle of the sheep, I wasn't afraid of anything."

Sheep and goat meat are staples for the Navajo. The internal organs, filled with vitamins and minerals, compensate for a limited supply of green vegetables in the Navajo diet. (Green peppers, used in this recipe, were introduced from Mexico by the Spanish.)

Raising sheep and goats remains an important economic activity for the Navajo. The sale of lambs, pelts, and wool—raw or woven—provides cash. But young children today are often away at school and are not available to herd the flocks, and young adults seek wage work. Thus, herding has become the work of older couples, who sometimes care for sheep from several households.

Melt butter in a large skillet, and sauté lamb until cooked through. Add tomatoes, bread crumbs, onion, coriander seed, cumin, and salt and pepper. Carefully remove tops and seeds from peppers and fill with lamb mixture.

Bake in a preheated 350° F. oven for 1 hour, or until peppers are tender. If desired, place peppers under broiler for a few seconds to brown tops. Sprinkle with fresh cilantro and serve hot or at room temperature. Serves 4

Turkeys have played varied roles in Pueblo life. The Anasazi kept turkeys at the backs of caves as early as A.D. 500, using the fluffy cloud-like breast feathers ceremonially and twisting the larger feathers to weave a cloth as warm as fur. This use of turkey feathers for warmth continued until the Spanish brought sheep to the Southwest. On August 3, 1540, shortly after the explorer Francisco Vásquez de Coronado entered into what is now New Mexico, he wrote to the Viceroy Antonio de Mendoza in Spain: "We found fowls, but only a few, and yet there are some. The Indians tell me that they do not eat these in any of the seven villages [Zuñi] but they keep them merely for the sake of procuring feathers. I do not believe this because they are very good, and better than those of Mexico."

Exactly four centuries later, in 1940, the anthropologist Elsie Clew Parsons wrote from New Mexico: "Buffalo was hunted from Taos [Pueblo] and, of course, eaten; and bear and wild turkey, not eaten elsewhere, are said to be eaten there. I have my doubts about bear, but domestic turkey I have seen Taos men eat, much to my surprise, for south for Taos, turkey is a ritual bird, kept that its feathers may be used in prayer offerings; and it would not be eaten, people say, even in times of famine."

9- to 12-pound turkey
   Salt and ground pepper,
   to taste
1 recipe Piñon-Raisin
   Stuffing
3 tablespoons melted
   butter or corn oil
1 to 2 teaspoons chili
   powder (preferably New
   Mexican red)
1 onion, peeled and halved
2 celery tops
⅓ cup unbleached flour

PUEBLO ROAST TURKEY WITH PIÑON-RAISIN STUFFING

The turkey appears in Pueblo and Navajo mythology as friend, helper, and provider of seeds. During their Corn Dances of late autumn, Zuñi kachinas give young boys feathered bows and arrows, and young girls kachina dolls with small loaves of bread in the form of deer, antelope, rabbits, and turkey. Bows and arrows symbolize the hunt, while dolls and loaves symbolize homemaking. At Cochiti Pueblo, a pregnant woman may wear a turkey feather in her belt to ensure that her child will be born with luxuriant hair. By taking the hair of little children in their beaks and pulling it, turkeys have the power to make hair grow.

Preheat oven to 325° F. Remove giblets and neck from turkey and reserve for broth. Rinse turkey and pat dry. Rub inside and out with salt and pepper. Stuff neck and body cavities loosely with Piñon-Raisin Stuffing and truss. Place in a shallow roasting pan. Combine butter and chili and brush over bird. Roast, allowing 20 minutes per pound, basting occasionally with butter and pan drippings until juices run clear, with no hint of pink when thigh is pierced.

While turkey is roasting, place neck and giblets, except liver, in a saucepan with onion, celery tops, and 5 cups of water. Chop liver and reserve. Over medium heat, bring water to a boil. Reduce heat to medium-low and simmer, uncovered, for about 40 minutes, until giblets are tender. Strain broth and reserve. Chop neck meat and giblets and reserve with liver.

Remove cooked turkey to a serving platter and keep warm. Pour pan juices into a 1-quart heat-proof measuring cup or bowl. Skim off 6 tablespoons of clear fat from top of juices and return fat to roasting pan. Skim off and discard any remaining fat, reserving degreased juices. Add flour to roasting pan and cook over medium heat, stirring, for 3 to 4 minutes, until flour is browned. Stir in reserved giblets and sauté briefly. Gradually add degreased pan juices and enough giblet broth to make 3½ cups total liquid. Cook, stirring over medium heat for 2 to 3 minutes, until gravy is thickened. Serve turkey with dressing and gravy. Serves 8 to 10

PIÑON-RAISIN STUFFING

6 cups cubed, day-old Adobe Bread or Italian bread
½ cup butter
1½ cups chopped onion
¾ cup chopped celery
1 cup piñon nuts (pignoli)
½ cup raisins
1 large egg, beaten
1¼ teaspoons crumbled dried sage
1¼ teaspoons salt
½ teaspoon ground pepper
1 to 2 tablespoons water (optional)

Preheat oven to 325° F. While it is heating, place bread cubes on a baking sheet and dry in oven for 10 to 15 minutes. Transfer bread to a large mixing bowl and reserve.

Melt butter in a large skillet and add onion and celery. Cook over medium-low heat, stirring often, for 3 to 4 minutes, until translucent. Stir in piñon nuts and raisins. Sauté until nuts are golden. Add to bread cubes and toss. Add egg and seasonings and toss again. For a moister stuffing, add 1 to 2 tablespoons water. Use stuffing to loosely stuff turkey. Place any remaining stuffing in a baking dish and bake separately.

Pedro de Castañeda, who accompanied Coronado to the Southwest in the 1540s, mentions in his letters to Spain that native cooks used juniper berries and coriander seeds and that the men hunted wild boar. But it was the Spanish who brought domesticated pigs from Spain to the Southwest. Similarly, chili pequin, a very hot small chili, grows wild on bushes in southern New Mexico and Arizona, and was long used by the Papago and Pima. However, the domesticated varieties of chilies that we know today were brought to the Southwest by the Spanish from Mexico, along with bell peppers and tomatoes.

Chocolate, according to Toltec legend, was stolen from the gods and given to the Indians of Mexico by Quetzalcoatl, their brother and ruler, because of his love for the people. He planted cocoa trees, and when the mature branches hung heavy, he collected the dark fruit and toasted it, showing the women how to beat it with water in gourds. At first, chocolate was reserved for priests and nobles, who drank the sacred liquid bitter. In later times, the Indians mixed it with honey. The Spanish added sugar and milk, and drank it hot. Chocolate traveled north with them to New Mexico and Arizona, and was incorporated into Pueblo cooking.

PUEBLO BARBECUED PORK ROAST

¼ cup vegetable oil or lard

1½ cups chopped onions

3 cloves garlic, minced

4 dried juniper berries, crushed

½ teaspoon crushed coriander seed

1 bay leaf

4 large ripe tomatoes, quartered and seeded

1¼ cups water

⅔ cup cider vinegar

⅓ to ½ cup honey

1 tablespoon ground chili, preferably New Mexican red

1 dried, medium-hot, New Mexican red chili, crushed

2 teaspoons salt

1 1-ounce square unsweetened chocolate, grated

4- to 5-pound pork rib roast

Heat oil in a large, heavy saucepan and sauté onions over medium heat until soft. Add garlic, juniper berries, coriander seed, and bay leaf and sauté for 2 to 3 minutes longer. Add tomatoes, water, vinegar, honey, ground chili, crushed chili, and salt. Simmer, covered, for 30 minutes. Add chocolate and simmer, uncovered, for 20 to 30 minutes, until the sauce is fairly thick.

Preheat the oven to 350° F. Place roast, fat side up, in a roasting pan and baste generously with sauce. Roast for about 3 hours, or until a meat thermometer inserted in the thickest part of roast (away from the bone) registers 175° F. Baste occasionally with sauce and pan drippings during roasting. Allow roast to sit for 10 minutes in a warm place before carving. Slice and spoon additional sauce over each serving. Serves 6 to 8

1 medium-sized rabbit,
approximately 4 pounds

2 tablespoons vegetable oil

¾ cup chopped onion

4 cups chicken broth and
4 cups water (or use a
total of 8 cups water)

1 cup red wine vinegar

1 tablespoon medium-hot
ground New Mexican red
chili

Salt, to taste

½ cup yellow cornmeal or
ground sunflower seeds

Tortillas or Adobe Bread,
for serving

PUEBLO RABBIT

Cut rabbit into serving pieces. Heat oil in a heavy Dutch oven and brown rabbit pieces well. Add onion, broth, water, vinegar, and chili. Simmer, partially covered, for 1½ hours, until rabbit is tender. Season with salt. Slowly pour in cornmeal, stirring constantly. Let simmer, uncovered, for an additional 10 to 15 minutes, until sauce is slightly thickened. Serve with tortillas or Adobe Bread.

Serves 4

Although venison was prized, rabbits were the major source of meat for the Southwestern tribes. Traditional hunting methods included throwing wooden rabbit sticks—similar to boomerangs—from a distance and using small hand-held clubs.

Ceremonial rabbit hunts were organized by each pueblo to provide food for ritual feasts. After prayers and offerings, the men would make fires in an area where rabbits were plentiful, gradually encircling the animals. During Kachina dances at Santa Domingo Pueblo, for example, ritually hunted rabbit was fed to the Storm Cloud Kachinas and to the leaders of the Kachina cult before every ritual feast. The Cacique, the highest priest in the pueblo, was given rabbit meat to feed his fetishes, which were his objects of supernatural potency.

At Cochiti Pueblo, some rabbit hunts were social events during which young women carried toy rabbit sticks as they accompanied the men. When a rabbit fell, the first woman who ran to it would receive it from the hunter. Later, she presented him with cooked food, and courtship would sometimes follow. Before the advent of rifles, rabbit sticks were carried by men and boys whenever they left the pueblo, in case rabbits or other small game should appear.

In the Southwest, sweet spine-covered cactus fruit, called *tunas*, are always available no matter how dry the season. Although several types of cacti, such as prickly pear, produce edible fruit, the giant saguaro cactus used by the Papago provides the meatiest fruit. These huge plants, many over twelve feet tall, create a desert forest of branches, which often resembles giant fantastic figures. The fruit grow at the very top and are picked in early morning or late afternoon to avoid the blazing sun.

The internal structure of the cactus is formed of vertical ribs around which the flesh grows. When a saguaro dies and nothing remains but ribs, these long, thin poles are used as fruit hooks. On one end a short stick is tied at an angle. This is used to snag the stem of the fruit and pull it loose. Some fallen fruit may break, revealing a dark red, jelly-like interior full of seeds. Others will have to be cut, through the hard, thorn-covered shell to reach the tender flesh.

As the first cactus begins to ripen, new fruit appears in abundance, but soon spoils in the desert heat. The Papago must quickly harvest this fruit and either dry or cook it. When cooked, the pulp is strained through baskets; only the juice comes through. A sweet jam is made of the remaining pulp. The juice is cooked down to a syrup and stored in jars.

During rainmaking feasts, to "pull down the clouds," the syrup is mixed with water and kept for two nights and a day near a warm fire. When the brew bubbles as strong as cider, it is drunk "as the earth drinks rain."

In modern times, jelly is often made from the cactus juice.

6 to 10 red-ripe prickly pear cactus fruits (enough to make 3½ cups of juice)
½ cup lemon juice
4½ cups sugar
1 3-fluid-ounce package liquid fruit pectin

CACTUS FRUIT JELLY

Carefully remove thorns from fruit by wiping with a paper towel and then brushing with a vegetable brush under water. Put fruit in a saucepan with enough water to cover. Boil for 15 to 20 minutes. Pour off water and discard. Mash or puree fruit through a strainer lined with doubled cheesecloth. Strain juice into a large measuring cup. Let juice sit for at least 30 minutes to allow sediment to settle to the bottom. Pour off juice carefully. You should have 3½ cups.

In a saucepan combine fruit juice, lemon juice, and sugar. Bring to a boil and boil 1 minute. Stir in pectin and boil for 1 minute longer. Remove from heat. Stir and skim foam off the top. Spoon into sterilized jelly jars and seal.

Makes 3 cups

Opposite: Feast Day Cookies and Paselitos

The Pueblo Indians give much attention to food, especially on Feast Days, when they must feed their families, a circle of friends, and even casual visitors. Field parties for planting or harvesting, kiva parties, a Kachina or Corn Dance, an initiation or wedding, the pueblo's Saint's Day—all require elaborate food preparation. In the Pueblo world, the households of men engaged in any ceremonial activity are the busiest, and at the conclusion of the feast, leftovers are distributed and carried home.

Pueblo hospitality is identified, as everywhere, with food; under no circumstances may one refuse food or, asking for it, be refused. To a caller from the vicinity, watermelon, piñon, or peaches will be offered, and it is proper to eat before announcing the reason for the visit. For visitors from far away, whenever they arrive, a regular meal will be served. To be stingy with food is unacceptable.

Visitors on Feast Days might be offered these special cookies, but we doubt there are ever any leftovers to be carried home.

FEAST DAY COOKIES

⅔ cup plus ¼ cup sugar

⅔ cup lard or vegetable shortening

1 egg

2 cups unbleached flour, sifted

4½ teaspoons baking powder

½ teaspoon vanilla extract

½ teaspoon anise seed

⅓ cup milk

½ cup piñon nuts (pignoli), chopped

1 teaspoon ground cinnamon

Preheat oven to 350° F. In a mixing bowl, cream ⅔ cup sugar and lard. Add egg and blend thoroughly. Stir in flour, baking powder, vanilla, and anise seed, blending thoroughly. Gradually add milk until a stiff dough is formed. Mix in the piñon nuts. Roll dough out on a lightly floured board to ½-inch thickness. Cut into 2-inch cookies with cookie cutter. Sprinkle tops with mixture of the remaining sugar and cinnamon. Bake cookies on a well-greased baking sheet for about 15 minutes, or until golden. Cool on a rack.
Makes 2 dozen 2-inch cookies

Sweet-tasting food was a special treat for the Pueblo people, who had no sugar until European contact. Wildflowers, berries, and cactus fruit provided some sweetness but the sugar in corn—from which we derive corn syrup today— became a source of sweetness through an ingenious method that the Indians developed. Young girls with "fresh, clean mouths," were chosen to chew a little fine-ground cornmeal. The chemical reaction of their saliva enzymes on the cornstarch produced sugar. Added to batter, this sweetness was enjoyed in various breads and cakes. Later, the juicy peaches and apricots brought by the Spanish to the Southwest added another versatile sweetener to Pueblo cooking. Small fruit pies became special foods, prized by visitors on feast days.

Filling:

1 cup dried fruit, cooked and drained (see Note)

⅓ cup sugar

1 tablespoon honey

¼ teaspoon ground cinnamon

Mash the cooked fruit and add sugar, honey, and cinnamon. Stir well.

Note: Any dried fruit, such as apricots, peaches, pears, currants, prunes, or raisins, may be used.

At the Santo Domingo Corn Dance in the summer of 1990, a feast was held to honor the Saint. Along with bowls of lamb stew, roast goat, salads, and breads, were many small fruit pies—all laid out under a shady ramada for the visiting crowds—an expression of expansive Pueblo hospitality. Anglos at the feast for the first time seemed surprised, but soon were enjoying the spread. One might remember the San Juan tale: when Flower-Bird found his missing wife at her parent's house, her mother urged: "Do not be ashamed, Flower-Bird, you are in a new house; eat well."

Dough:

1½ cups unbleached flour

1 teaspoon baking powder

½ teaspoon salt

6 tablespoons lard or vegetable shortening, chilled

3 to 4 tablespoons cold water

1 egg

1 tablespoon milk

PASELITOS (LITTLE FRUIT PIES)

Preheat oven to 400° F. Combine flour, baking powder, and salt in a mixing bowl. Cut in lard until mixture resembles fine meal. Slowly add water until dough is easy to roll. Roll out to ¼-inch thickness and cut into 4-inch rounds. Put 1 tablespoon of fruit filling on one half of each round, fold over the other half of the round, and pinch edges together firmly. Prick the tops in several places with the tines of a fork. Mix egg with milk and brush on the tops of the pies. Bake for 15 minutes or until lightly browned. Makes 10 Paselitos

Wheat was introduced to Pueblo farmers by the Spanish three centuries ago. It was readily adopted because, unlike corn for which each kernel must be planted deep within the earth with a digging stick, wheat may be broadcast. *Panocha*, made with sprouted wheat meal, derives from an old Spanish recipe that has become part of Pueblo Indian cooking. At San Juan Pueblo, it is served at Easter.

If sprouted wheat flour is not available at markets in your area, you can make your own by placing wheat purchased at a health food store in a jar with water to cover for 24 hours. Drain the wheat and spread out on a clean cloth to sprout. When the grain sprouts, it should be dried, ground into flour, and sifted.

Traditionally, this dessert is sweetened with piloncillos, pyramid-shaped brown sugar lumps that are available in most of the Southwest.

PANOCHA (SPROUTED WHEAT PUDDING)

2 cups sprouted wheat meal

1 cup whole wheat flour

4½ cups boiling water

2 piloncillos or ½ cup brown sugar

¼ cup granulated sugar

1½ tablespoons butter

¼ teaspoon ground cinnamon (optional)

1 teaspoon vanilla extract (optional)

Heavy cream, for serving

Combine wheat meal and flour in a mixing bowl. Add 3½ cups boiling water to make a thick paste; cover and let stand. Place piloncillos in a bowl with remaining cup of boiling water to dissolve. Place granulated sugar in a heavy saucepan and stir over low heat until lightly caramelized. Add brown sugar syrup to saucepan and stir in butter, cinnamon, and vanilla. Preheat oven to 300° F. Place wheat mixture in a buttered 2-quart, oven-proof dish. Stir in hot syrup and bake for about 2 hours, until pudding is thick and dark brown. Serve warm with heavy cream.
Serves 6 to 8

NAVAJO PEACH CRISP

There were no peaches in the Southwest until early in the seventeenth century, when Spanish priests planted them in their orchards. For the Hopi, who had no sugar, peaches were a delight. They began to cultivate them, drying them in the sun as they had done with yucca fruit. These dried peaches became valued items of trade, especially with the neighboring Navajo.

According to legend, after some Navajo moved westward and settled in Canyon de Chelly, near the Hopi mesas, the Hopi crops failed. A starving Hopi woman came to the Navajo to beg for food, bringing with her the knowledge of peach planting. She later married into the tribe and taught the Navajo to dry and plant peach seeds in sheltered areas of the canyon's high cliffs, which reflected the heat of the sun and kept winds away. These extensive Navajo peach orchards were destroyed by Kit Carson when he forced the Navajo from the canyon in 1864. Today, canned peaches, pears, and fruit cocktail—obtained at the trading posts—are much enjoyed.

6 large ripe peaches,
   peeled, pitted, and sliced
   (5 to 6 cups)
¼ cup granulated sugar
½ teaspoon cinnamon
   (optional)
¾ cup unbleached flour
¾ cup light brown sugar
¼ teaspoon salt
½ cup butter
2 tablespoons piñon nuts
   (pignoli) (optional)

Preheat oven to 375° F. In a 1½- to 2-quart baking dish, toss the peaches with granulated sugar and cinnamon. In a mixing bowl, combine flour, brown sugar, and salt. Cut in butter until the mixture resembles coarse meal. Sprinkle this mixture evenly over the peaches. Sprinkle the top with nuts. Bake for 30 to 40 minutes, until golden brown on top.
Serves 4 to 6

Sweet bread puddings are a favorite in the Pueblo villages. Before sugar was available, the batter was sweetened by adding either a starter—dough pre-chewed by young girls—or a mixture of dried flowers. Portions were wrapped in green corn leaves, which added additional sweetness, and then boiled.

At Nambe, as in other pueblos, the term "governor" has in interesting history. Traditionally, the leader among the pueblos (called the *cacique* by the Spanish) is concerned with the welfare of the whole community. He leads a life of strict ritual observance and is totally immersed in the annual round of religious ceremonies. He holds his office for life, and appoints the other village officers.

PUEBLO GOVERNOR'S PUDDING

½ cup raisins

1 cup hot water

6 slices Adobe Bread or toasting white bread

2 eggs, beaten

¾ cup dark brown sugar

1 teaspoon vanilla extract

1 teaspoon cinnamon

½ cup shredded longhorn or Cheddar cheese

½ cup light cream

The Spanish created a new framework for the community with a different hierarchy of beliefs and human relations, with the King of Spain recognized as owner of the land and the source of all authority. To this end, when Juan de Oñate set up his first capital in San Juan Pueblo, he simultaneously appointed governors (*gobernadores*) in each district. Indians who were cooperative were given appointments; a cane was their badge of office. The Eastern Pueblos accepted this simply as an adjunct to their existing village government. The *gobernadores* became go-betweens with the Spanish, but were under strict control of the *cacique*; their roles were limited to interactions with Spanish and other outsiders. Today the governors act as the liaison between the pueblos and visitors, and are responsible for village protocol. Perhaps this rich bread pudding was intended as a reward for their efforts.

Preheat oven to 350° F. Soak raisins in hot water. Toast bread slices and allow to cool. Add beaten eggs, sugar, vanilla, and cinnamon to raisins. Alternately layer bread, cheese, and raisin mixture in a 2-quart baking dish. Pour cream over all and bake for 30 minutes, or until all the liquid has been absorbed and pudding is firm. Serve warm or at room temperature.
Serves 6 to 8

Isleta, a pueblo in central New Mexico, has outstanding orchards where many families have planted peach and apricot trees. When the fruit is ripe, the families camp in the orchards for days, cutting the peaches and apricots in half and spreading them out to dry in the sun. The dried fruits are called "ears" in many Pueblo languages because they resemble human ears.

The rich custard-based rice puddings served in the pueblos can be traced back to old Spanish recipes. Isleta cooks include dried apricots in their own elegant version.

FANCY ISLETA PUEBLO RICE PUDDING

¼ **cup raw rice**

 3 **cups light cream**

½ **cup dried apricots,**
   chopped

½ **cup sugar**

½ **teaspoon salt**

½ **teaspoon cinnamon**

3 **eggs**

1 **teaspoon vanilla extract**

Preheat oven to 325° F. Wash rice. In a large saucepan, combine rice with cream, apricots, sugar, salt, and cinnamon. Simmer, stirring often, over medium-low heat for about 20 minutes, until rice is tender. Separate eggs into 2 large mixing bowls.

Whisk hot cream mixture into yolks and place in the top of a double boiler. Cook, stirring constantly, over simmering water until custard is thick enough to coat the back of a spoon. Stir in vanilla and remove from heat. Beat whites until soft peaks form. Add half of the whites to custard and combine well.

Gently fold in remaining whites. Pour mixture into a 2-quart baking or soufflé dish. Bake for 40 to 50 minutes, or until pudding is puffed and lightly browned on top and custard is just set. Serves 6

Coiled strips of pumpkin and melon drying in the sun were a common sight at Zuñi at the turn of the century. Simmered, often together with dried peaches and, if available, added sugar, they made a popular dessert.

Pumpkin candy is another old Pueblo treat. Traditionally the strips of pumpkin in this recipe are soaked in a bath of water and wood ashes to soften. Today many Indian cooks substitute baking soda for the ashes. Those who prefer a less sweet candy sometimes add lemon juice and thin strips of lemon zest to the sugar syrup and flavor their syrup with cilantro. If you have a really sweet tooth, roll the dried candy in coarse sugar.

PUEBLO PUMPKIN CANDY

2- to 3-pound pumpkin
1½ teaspoons baking soda
2½ cups sugar
½ cup water
  Juice and zest of 1 small
  lemon (optional)
3 to 4 sprigs fresh cilantro
  (optional)

Peel and seed pumpkin and cut it into 2×4-inch strips. Stir baking soda into enough water to cover strips. Add pumpkin strips and let stand 12 hours. Drain and rinse pumpkin in running water. Drop strips into a pot of boiling water and cook until tender but not soft. Remove pumpkin strips, crisp in ice cold water, and drain.

Combine sugar with ½ cup water, lemon juice and zest, and cilantro in a saucepan. Heat, stirring, until sugar is dissolved, then boil slowly without stirring for 10 minutes. Add pumpkin strips, cover the pot, and simmer for about 20 minutes until syrup is thick and strips are brittle. Spread candy out on a rack or on a wax paper-covered tray to dry for at least 10 hours. Roll in additional sugar if desired and store in an airtight container. Makes about 1 pound

THE

WEST

THE WEST

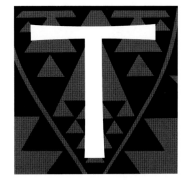

The quest for food, whether obtained by hunting, gathering, fishing, or farming, was always a central concern to Native American peoples. Each individual was involved in subsistence activities, and all were largely dependent on nature's bounty, which could be extended generously or inexplicably withheld. Among the tribes whose large amounts of food meant wealth, the Northwest Coast peoples were the richest of all. They lived where the sea abounded in food, where there were many animals on land, and where a rainy, temperate climate allowed a wide variety of useful plants to flourish. Located along the coasts of Oregon, Washington, British Columbia, and Southeast Alaska, with some groups settled on the Queen Charlotte Islands and Vancouver Island, their large-scale economic activities—the "harvesting" of wild food—became the basis for one of the most complex native cultures in North America.

However, for the tribes that lived to the east of the coast and across the mountains into the Plateau region, or to the south in California and the adjacent Great Basin, survival was a time-consuming challenge. In these three areas, hunting and fishing could only supplement the major food sources—roots in the Plateau, acorns in California, and wild plants, roots, and seeds in the Great Basin.

Plateau people—the Sanpoil, Kutenai, Klamath, Flathead, and Nez Percé—depended on salmon that passed through the tributaries of the Fraser and Columbia rivers. But camas roots, relatives of the lily and onion, were their staple. This bulb-like vegetable was eaten raw, roasted, and boiled, or ground into meal, made into cakes, and stored for use in winter.

In California, the Hupa, Pomo, Mohave, Yuki, and Luiseno used acorns from six species of oak as a highly nutritious staple food, once they discovered how to leach out their bitter tannic acid. This rich and reliable harvest, together with many edible wild plants, such as nuts, seeds, berries, fruits, and greens, as well as deer, elk, and rabbits, led to a greatly expanded population. The California tribes also enjoyed army worms (small, hairless caterpillars) that were dried in the sun for use in winter, grasshoppers, hornet and yellow jacket grubs, and angleworms. Salmon and other fish were available along the shores and in the streams.

The Great Basin, an area of low range surrounded by high mountains, including the Cascades and Sierra Nevadas, is home to the Ute, Paiute, Shoshone, Gosiute, and Bannock tribes. Here, mountains as high as 13,000 feet block the rain from the west, although some rain flows into the basin, creating small oases in a desert-like environment. Few places in the world have so few edible resources, but the people became expert in identifying and using food plants, especially roots. Edible bulbs were collected and dried for winter. They gathered roots of young bulrushes (or tules), shoots of thistle, squaw cabbage, clover, and pulpy cactus leaves. There was no staple food; piñon might have served, but the trees yield an unpredictable crop once every three or four years. Grasshoppers, crickets, caterpillars, ants, and locusts—along with their eggs, larvae, and chrysalides—were all enjoyed as food.

In this chapter, we focus on the tribes of the Northwest Coast, part of a well-defined cultural entity, vital and inventive, that has been described as "the most elaborate nonagricultural society in the world." These Native Americans occupy a long narrow strip of rugged terrain extending some 1,500 miles along the Pacific shoreline, from southeastern Alaska to northern California. The rocky wooded shores of the mainland plus thousands of islands, broken by innumerable bays, inlets, and fjords, are exposed to the constant winds and tides of the Pacific. Glacier-hung mountains, often capped by clouds, rise steeply along much of the coast. Lush deep-green forests of cedar, fir, hemlock, and spruce, often shrouded in mist, grow down to the water's edge. Rainfall, clouds, and fog are frequent, the result of water vapor carried eastward by prevailing Pacific winds. Warmed by the Japanese Current, which flows offshore, these winds help maintain a year-round temperate climate in the region.

In this moist, gray-green landscape, brightened by brief periods of warm summer sunlight, twenty-eight tribes from seven linguistic families, known collectively as Northwest Coast Indians, once built villages with huge, rectangular cedar-plank houses that sheltered extended families of forty members or more. The northern tribal grouping includes the Haida, Tlingit, Tsimshian, and Bella Bella; among the southern tribes are the Kwakiutl, Nootka, and Salish. Their villages, many with imposing totem poles facing the sea, were built along beaches protected by the rocky outcroppings of the shore, and on the banks of glacier-fed rivers and streams. Their descendants live here today, and, as did their ancestors, they rely heavily on the sea: fishing, hunting sea mammals, and collecting shellfish. Herring, smelts, and five kinds of salmon make their way up streams, while halibut, seals, sea otters, and—on occasion—whales can be caught in the ocean. Receding tides provide clams, mussels, oysters, abalone, limpets, and crabs. An old adage claims "When the tide goes out, the table is set."

Fish return from the sea to the rivers during spring and summer, with five to seven salmon "runs" each season. In spring, schools of eulachon, a kind of smelt that is sometimes called candlefish, appear. They are so rich in oil that if a wick is strung through one, it can serve as a candle. Fishing was a full-time activity, and men worked day and night during the season. But such quantities of fish would be of little use unless they could be stored for winter. Women cleaned the fish on shore, working quickly to preserve a food that would otherwise rapidly spoil. Vast amounts were smoked, dried, pressed, and packed in oil for year-round use. In addition, seasonal hunting on land provided ducks, geese, deer, elk, and bear, although their meat was less valued than that of the oil-rich fish. Moreover, the coast people dreaded the dark, tangled forests behind the villages, where legends told of dangerous spirits, especially in winter. Those who hunted in the forest were looked upon with awe; these hunters would invoke personal helping spirits, and sing special songs to appease the animals.

In addition to drying fish and preparing meat, the women gathered basketfuls of the many species of berries that grow in the moist coastal soil, including salmonberry, huckleberry, gooseberry, black currant, Oregon grape, and bearberry. They would roast, dry, and store soft roots, including fern, lupine, and rush, and pound the all-important camas root into a starchy flour that provided an equivalent of bread for the long winter ahead.

Camas grows wild in meadows and on grassy bluffs. It has grass-like leaves, blue blossoms, and bulbs as much as an inch across. The bulbs were dug with sticks, with the small ones left in the ground to mature the following season. Harvesting was a labor-intensive, and therefore cooperative, enterprise. Some women picked bulbs, others baked them in pit ovens dug in the camas field, and yet others loaded the baked roots into baskets to be subsequently sun-dried and stored for winter.

Loaves made from camas flour could be kept all winter, and were eaten with fish oil or seal oil. When steamed, the starchy bulbs became sugary. The camas supplemented a diet otherwise low in carbohydrates and, as a result, became an important item of trade for the Northwest Coast people. When supplies became low, men would take canoes into the ocean for halibut and cod.

Higher living standards are traditionally associated with intensive agriculture, which leads to increased population and leisure time. However, the complex Northwest Coast culture was developed by a hunting and gathering people. The foods from the water and coastal lands provided the Indians with an ecological equivalent to agriculture; they "harvested" food much the way farmers harvest crops.

Salmon was available in unbelievable quantities—they were so numerous that they could fill the rivers from bank to bank as they swam upstream to spawn. Many observed that "you could walk across on their backs." The return of the first salmon was greeted with a sacred rite of thanksgiving. This Kwakiutl prayer is recited by the wife of the fisherman who catches the first salmon:

O supernatural ones! O swimmers! I thank you that you are willing to come to us. Protect us from danger that nothing evil may happen to us when we eat you. Supernatural ones! . . . For that is the reason you come here that we may catch you for food. We know that only your bodies are dead here, but your souls come to watch over us when we are going to eat what you have given us. . . .

Opposite: Whipped Raspberries and Honey

The copious food supply, the techniques perfected for its preservation, and the forests of great cedars, which provided material for daily needs, from housing and tools to clothing, helped form the distinctive character of Northwest Coast culture. Here the people developed powerful and sophisticated artistic traditions and elaborate religious, social, and political systems. Chiefdoms and social classes were validated by public display of status symbols. Events—including marriages between important families, the birth of an heir, the construction of a chief's house, naming ceremonies, girls' puberty rites, initiations into secret societies, the raising of a totem pole, the death of a chief and the accession of a new one, the tattooing of a chief's children—all were acknowledged at great feasts. Called "potlatch," a name from the Chinook meaning "gift," such ceremonies also established the status of lesser group members, and confirmed their rights to fishing and berry-gathering areas and certain names and ceremonial objects.

Entire villages might be invited, with the potlatch guests traveling in dugouts (cedar canoes). After days of lavish feasting, dramatic performances by masked dancers, and formal speeches and announcements, the hosts distributed gifts—an essential element of the potlatch—to the guests, which included carved and painted cedar-plank chests filled with dried fish and berries, barrels of fish and seal oil, piles of woven blankets and mats, sometimes even furs and jewelry. The guests departed, laden with gifts, and determined, as was the custom, to produce an even greater potlatch in their own village.

A potlatch involved all the people, reaffirming the structure of Northwest Coast society. It encouraged the creation of large food stores—potlatch preparations could take several years—and the sharing of food in a regulated way. For a village in which the salmon run had failed, or where lingering dense fog had prevented fishing, a potlatch invitation from some more fortunate neighbors was especially welcome; the situation might one day be reversed. But this native way of life was not to remain untouched.

Captain James Cook, who arrived at Nootka Sound in 1778, suggested that a profitable fur trade could be established along the Northwest Coast. By 1792, European trading ships brought new products: metal tools, guns, woolen blankets, kitchen utensils, fabrics, and trinkets, many of which became gifts at ever more elaborate potlatch feasts. By the 1800s, a land-based fur trade was established by the Hudson's Bay Company and others. Fort Vancouver became a center where traps and guns were available to anyone. As men abandoned traditional methods of obtaining furs, the guardian hunting spirits were no longer an essential part of their lives, the potlatch began losing its earlier functions, and the social fabric of tribal life weakened. Tragically, European-introduced smallpox and measles, to which the native people had no immunity, caused the deaths of many thousands. Villages broke up. Covered wagons arrived with increasing numbers of settlers, eager to farm the land, to cut down trees for lumber, and to build mills, and roads and schools. There was no place for the native people to go.

By 1860, most of the Northwest Coast people lived on reservations. Those aspects of daily life that once centered around fishing were gone. Government attempts to turn the Indians into farmers had little success; those who did succeed met increasing numbers of homesteaders and were forced off the land by soldiers. Many sought wage work as gatherers in commercial berry fields where, for a brief time, it was possible to revive a semblance of their earlier way of life. Others found employment in the lumber industry where they could feel at home in open encampments near the cedar forests.

Although the Northwest Coast people lost much of their traditional land, they never completely lost their connection to fishing and the sea. Today, one sees a cultural renaissance. Fleets of fishing boats are prominent features of their coastal villages. Some men work for commercial fisheries, while a number have formed logging cooperatives. Land claims and native fishing rights, guaranteed by treaties, are being aggressively pursued. Northwest Coast art is acclaimed around the world, and there is a new vigor among young artists. This rebirth is reviving cultural traditions and native languages. Potlatch, as a sharing ritual, is alive again. And, at Northwest Community College, which serves the coastal Indians of Washington State, tribal members can study the ways of commercial salmon fishing along with aspects of their traditional culture.

—Harriet Koenig

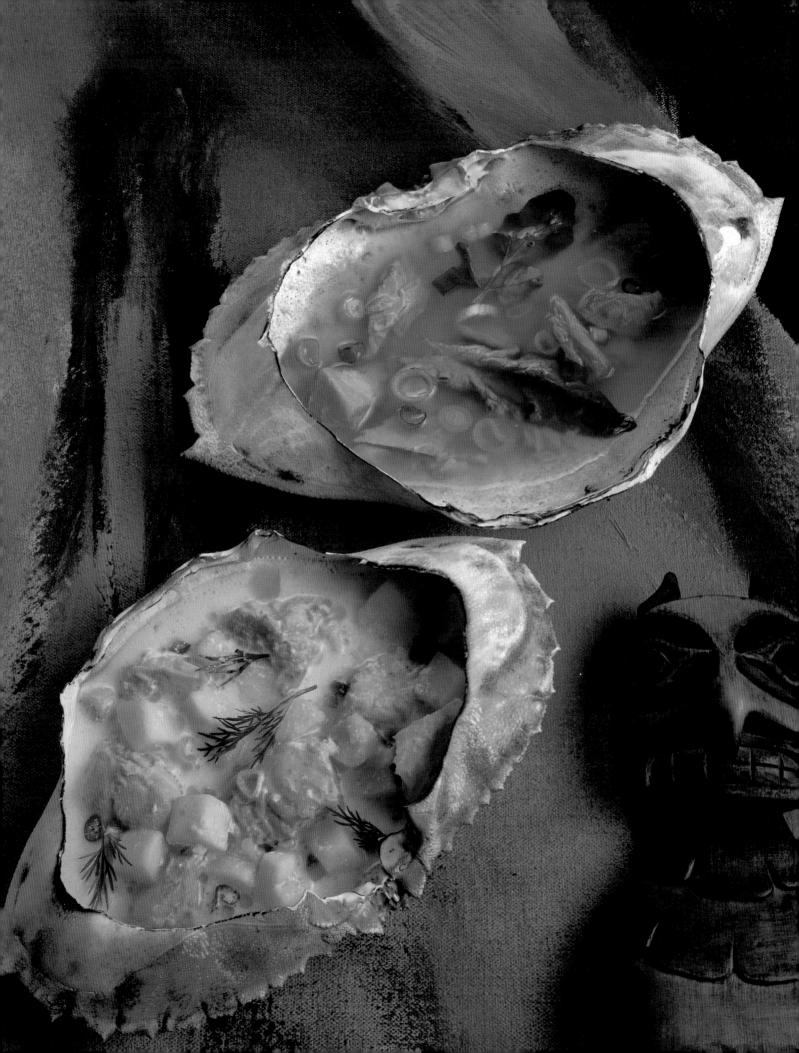

The seven species of Pacific salmon begin their lives in freshwater rivers and streams, sometimes as far as 1,500 miles from the ocean. Spawned from thousands of tiny eggs, salmon travel downstream to the open sea, where they remain for three or four years, fattening on zooplankton and small fish. In summer, when the females are ready to lay eggs, they return to their birthplaces. It is a long, arduous journey that requires swimming four or five miles a day, leaping over rocks and cascades, and eluding predators. Once there, each female, by thrashing her body about, digs a hollow in the riverbed and deposits her eggs, which are fertilized by a milky cloud of sperm from a nearby male. The

PACIFIC SALMON CHOWDER

female then sweeps a protective cover of gravel over the nest with her tail. Shortly afterwards, both parents die, spent from the trip of hundreds of miles over many weeks and the rigors of spawning.

Of these seven salmon species, "Five Tribes" return to the Northwest Coast: Chinook, Sockeye, Coho, Humpback, and Dog. Villagers closest to the ocean catch the fattest salmon, because the fish do not feed as they struggle upstream; villagers farther inland catch thinner, paler salmon. Down-river people claim to make the most delicious chowder, with fat fresh salmon, while those upriver say that salmon are best just before they have spawned, when they have used up most of their body fat and are better for drying.

Opposite: Pacific Salmon Chowder and Pacific Smoked Salmon Soup

1 tablespoon butter or vegetable oil
4 potatoes, peeled and diced
1 cup green onions, sliced
¼ teaspoon dill seed
6 cups milk
1 pound fresh salmon, cut into chunks
Salt and pepper, to taste
Dill sprigs, for garnish

Melt butter in a large saucepan over medium heat. Add potatoes, green onions, and dill seed, and sauté for 2 to 3 minutes. Add milk and simmer over low heat for 40 minutes. Add fresh salmon and simmer for 10 minutes more. Season with salt and pepper. Garnish individual servings with dill sprigs. Serves 6 to 8

PACIFIC SMOKED SALMON SOUP

In 1778, Captain Cook described the wooden boxes, small and large, that were used by the Nootka for cooking and serving.

> Boiling is performed in a wooden trough like an oblong box by putting red hot stones into the liquor, a heape of which always compose the fire hearth, they put them in and out of the pot with a kind of wooden tongs. In this manner, they boil all kinds of meat and make soups.

In 1789, Edward Dixon, a fur trader, visited the Haida of the Queen Charlotte Islands and described the stone-boiling technique, there used with baskets. Wetting kept the fibers swollen and the baskets watertight, making it possible to use them for preparing soup.

6 cups chicken broth

½ pound alder-smoked Pacific salmon

⅔ cup sliced green onions

Salt and pepper, to taste

½ cup watercress

½ cup small-leaf spinach

In a large saucepan, combine chicken broth, smoked salmon, and green onions. Bring to a boil. Reduce heat, cover, and simmer for 15 minutes. Season with salt and pepper and add watercress and spinach. Cook an additional 5 minutes.
Serves 6

When Lewis and Clark explored the Northwest Coast in the mid 1800s, they saw salmon swimming so thick that only a fraction could be harvested; traps and nets facing downstream filled within minutes. Each spring, villagers built weirs, high wooden fences across shallow salmon-packed streams. Platforms along the top allowed men to stand with long-handled nets, where they worked night and day, dipping up the salmon stopped by the weirs and piling them in canoes. Because there were thousands of fish, and the riverbeds often curved beneath the weirs, many salmon could continue upstream where other villages would catch their share. After the fish were dried and smoked they were stored in baskets to provide food for the rest of the year. Many found their way into smoked salmon soup.

After a tedious winter diet of dried fish and fish oil, Northwest Coast women eagerly anticipated the first green shoots of spring. Greens, roots, and nuts were savored fresh, or preserved for later use. Wild celery, purple clover roots and leaves, pigweed, salty tasting glasswort, wild rhubarb, dandelion greens, wild onions, wild spinach, and watercress all brought nutrients and variety to the bountiful table of the Northwest Coast tribes.

This recipe, using hazelnuts, greens, and fresh oysters, combines traditional foods in an excellent soup.

OYSTER-HAZELNUT SOUP

½ cup blanched, coarsely chopped toasted hazelnuts or filberts
¼ cup chopped onion
3 cups water
¾ cup shredded spinach, arugula, mâche, or watercress
½ pound small, raw, shucked oysters, with their liquor
1 cup heavy cream (optional)
Salt and pepper, to taste

Place hazelnuts, onion, and water in a saucepan and bring to a boil. Reduce heat to a simmer. Cover and cook for 30 minutes. Add greens and oysters, with their liquor, and simmer gently until edges of oysters have curled. Add cream, if desired, and cook to heat through. Season the soup with salt and pepper and serve hot.
Serves 4 to 6

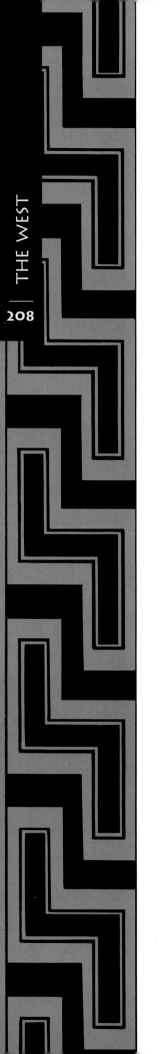

Green wild onions, which closely resemble chives and green onions, are eaten raw and cooked throughout North America. Along the Northwest Coast, these bulbs, harvested in spring, were also roasted, dried, and boiled in soup.

When John Jewitt of the ship *Boston* visited the Nootka in 1803, he stopped at the Yuquot village, a major port-of-call for American and European trading ships. The villagers had accumulated a rich supply of exotic trade goods. Jewitt mentions trading parties from other villages in his journals, noting as items of trade geese and ducks, sea otter skins, oil, whale sinew, salal-berry cakes, dentalia shells, red ochre, elk hides, and—most surprising—wild onions.

GREEN ONION SOUP

**12 to 14 green onions,
washed and sliced**
4 dried juniper berries
6 cups chicken broth
Salt and pepper, to taste

In a soup pot, combine the onions, juniper berries, and broth. Bring to a boil, then simmer for 30 to 40 minutes. Season with salt and pepper. Serves 6

6 cups fiddlehead ferns

2 to 3 tablespoons eulachon oil, melted butter, or olive oil

Salt and pepper, to taste

STEAMED FIDDLEHEAD FERNS

Indian women gathered many varieties of fern in spring. Fiddleheads, young curled fern fronds, have a fresh green taste, between broccoli and asparagus. The roots of ferns were used as a starchy vegetable, baked in embers and eaten on the spot or dried and powdered for use as flour in winter. Fern roots were so valued by Northwest Coast people, who lived in a region where starch was difficult to obtain, that the first ones roasted were reserved by the Kwakiutl for their chiefs.

Ferns served other purposes as well. The raw roots of bracken fern were chewed as a cough remedy. The Yakutat Tlingit used fern leaves as mats and for lining pits and vessels for cooking, and the Makah used the leaves as bedding when traveling. Ferns also played a role in the ritual welcoming ceremony for the first salmon, which could be cleaned only with the delicate fronds.

Fiddlehead ferns are prized by Native Americans of both coasts. They are now found fresh during May at better produce stores across the country, and are also available canned. In the Northwest, steamed or boiled fiddleheads are tossed with eulachon, or candlefish, oil. Since this oil is only available regionally—and is an acquired taste—melted butter or olive oil may be substituted.

Rinse fiddleheads and steam or blanch in boiling water for 3 to 4 minutes, until crisp-tender. Toss with eulachon oil, season with salt and pepper, and serve.
Serves 4 to 6

Beets are not native to the Americas. They may have been introduced to the Northwest Coast by Russian traders and settlers in the nineteenth century. Indians of the region traditionally included several native roots and tubers in their diet, and this newcomer was readily adopted.

Wild ginger *(Asarum canadense)*, sometimes called "Canadian snakeroot," was used as a seasoning and as a cure for indigestion by tribes all across the northern border of the United States. The plant has brownish flowers and grows in shady wooded areas. Both the blossoms and the root were boiled in water to form a gingery solution that was placed in the sun to evaporate until only a powder remained. Pieces of wild ginger root were also added directly to the cooking pot as a seasoning.

HONEY-GINGER BAKED BEETS

8 medium beets (about 2 pounds)
3 tablespoons butter or margarine
4 tablespoons honey
½ teaspoon ground ginger
Salt and pepper, to taste

Scrub beets well, but do not peel. Place them in a large saucepan, cover with water, and bring to a boil over high heat. Reduce heat to medium-low and simmer beets for 40 to 50 minutes, until just tender.

When cool enough to handle, peel beets and place them in an ovenproof baking dish. In a small saucepan, melt butter and mix in honey and ginger. Season sauce with salt and pepper and pour over beets. Cover and bake in a preheated 350°F. oven for 45 to 60 minutes, stirring occasionally, until beets are well glazed. Serves 4 to 6

1 cup watercress leaves and tender stems

1 cup lamb's-quarter (also called pitseed goosefoot or pigweed) or small spinach leaves and tender stems

1 cup miner's lettuce (also called Indian lettuce), mâche, or arugula

½ cup tender nasturtium and violet leaves and flowers

1 tablespoon honey

¼ cup cider vinegar

⅓ cup sunflower or corn oil

2 teaspoons chopped fresh mint or dill weed

Salt and pepper (optional)

Native Americans gathered many varieties of tender young wild cresses and other greens and flowers in the spring and early summer months, which they ate raw. Cultivated watercress, widely available today, is a hybridized descendant of these wild cresses. So are cultivated nasturtiums, which are also called Indian Cress. Wild greens such as lamb's-quarter, miner's lettuce, dandelion greens, and purslane are now sold in fancy produce stores across the country as "field lettuce," and are well worth trying.

WILD GREENS AND FLOWERS SALAD

Rinse greens and flowers and pat dry. In a salad bowl, combine honey and vinegar. Whisk in oil. Add mint and season to taste with salt and pepper. Add greens and flowers and toss gently. Serve immediately.
Serves 4 to 6

BUCKSKIN BREAD

The name Buckskin Bread is self-explanatory when you see the color of a baked loaf. This simple bread, popular with many Northwest Coast tribes, has a nice, fine-crumbed texture and a silky, light tan crust.

2 cups unbleached flour

1 teaspoon baking powder

1 teaspoon salt

1 cup water

Preheat oven to 400°F. Sift dry ingredients into a mixing bowl. Quickly mix in the water. Press dough into a greased 9-inch pie plate. Bake bread for about 30 minutes, until very lightly browned on top. Turn bread out and let cool on a rack. Makes 1 loaf

BANNOCK BREAD

The term "bannock" is used in different regions to describe different breads. The word itself is Scottish in origin and is thought to have come into use in the New World because of intermarriage between Native Americans and early Scottish and French traders. There is also a Bannock tribe, a people of Shoshonean stock related to the Northern Paiutes, who live in southern Idaho and western Wyoming. Members of this tribe wore their hair in a topknot that reminded white settlers of a loaf of bread.

Combine dry ingredients in a mixing bowl. Cut in shortening until mixture resembles coarse meal. Gradually mix in water to form a thick dough. Turn dough out onto a lightly floured surface and knead for 15 minutes, or until it is very smooth. Grease bottom and sides of a 10-inch cast-iron skillet. Press dough into the pan and cook, uncovered, on top of the stove over low heat for about 10 minutes on each side. Watch carefully so bread does not burn before center is cooked through. Place loaf on a rack to cool. Serves 6

2 cups unbleached flour

4 teaspoons baking powder

1 teaspoon salt

½ cup vegetable shortening

½ cup water

Place rose hips and enough water to cover in a large saucepan. Bring to a boil, reduce heat to a simmer, and cook, uncovered, until rose hips are soft enough to mash, adding more water as necessary. (This will take 20 to 45 minutes.)
Makes 2 cups

SKOKOMISH ROSE HIP PUREE

The wild rose is prized by Native Americans for its beauty and also for its usefulness as food and medicine. For the Shoshone of Wyoming, the rose is a favorite design for their beautiful beadwork. In the Southeast, the Cherokee use roses as a decorative motif and make rose petals into a delicate jelly.

Rose hips are used by many tribes to make a curative tea. The hips themselves are rich in vitamin C and the seeds are a good source of vitamin E. A traditional Crow recipe calls for combining pounded fresh rose hips with melted tallow and sugar. This mixture is formed into balls that are roasted on a stick like marshmallows as a special treat.

Bruce Miller, a chef associated with the Skokomish Tribal Council in Shelton, Washington, tells us that rose hip puree is used in the Northwest as a condiment with grilled salmon or meat and as a seasoning in soups and stews.

**4 cups fresh or dried
rose hips, seeded
4 to 6 cups water**

Combine dry ingredients in a mixing bowl. Mix together egg, milk, and honey and beat into dry ingredients to form a smooth batter. Stir in melted butter. Drop by tablespoonfuls onto a hot, greased griddle. Cook, turning each cake when it is browned on the underside and puffed and slightly set on top.

Note: For a description of another method of leaching tannin from acorns, see page 37.

Makes 12 to 15 griddle cakes

⅔ cup finely ground acorn meal or finely ground hazelnuts

⅓ cup unbleached flour

1 teaspoon baking powder

¼ teaspoon salt

1 egg, beaten

¾ cup milk

1 tablespoon honey

3 tablespoons melted butter

ACORN GRIDDLE CAKES

Although culturally similar to the Northwest Coast peoples, the Hupa, Karok, Miwok, Pomo, and Yurok of northern California differed in that acorns were a staple of their diet. When the nuts ripened in the fall, women collected a rich harvest in large conical baskets, assisted by men and boys who climbed the trees to shake the acorns down. The nuts were shelled, split, dried, and stored in the superbly woven baskets for which these tribes are renowned.

When flour was needed, acorns were stone-ground and the meal leached in a sand pit. Hot water was poured over the meal to dissolve the bitter tannin, which was absorbed in the sand below. Leached meal was made into soup, mush, bread, and small cakes. Hot, cooked, thickened acorn mush, placed in a small basket and cooled in a stream, formed a loaf the consistency of modern gelatin. Acorn griddle cakes, however, are especially appealing to the modern palate.

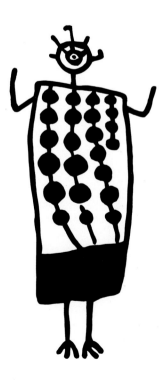

5 to 7 pounds of charcoal

1 8-pound wild Canada or domestic goose, dressed

2 teaspoons ground ginger
Salt and pepper

2 cups chopped, dried crab apples or other dried apples

1 cup dried cranberries (optional)

½ cup dried currants

1½ cups alder or apple wood chips, soaked in water (optional)

¾ cup brown sugar

2 tablespoons water

Prepare a charcoal grill (with cover) using about 5 pounds of charcoal. Rinse goose and pat dry. Remove any excess fat from the body cavity. If using a domestic goose, prick skin along the base of the breast and thighs so the fat will drain off. Rub goose with 1 teaspoon ginger and sprinkle lightly with salt and pepper. In a mixing bowl, combine dried fruits and remaining ginger. Stuff the body cavity with this mixture. Truss the goose. Arrange red-hot coals around a large drip pan. Sprinkle damp wood chips over the coals. Place goose on the grill, over the drip pan. Cover grill leaving all vents open. Cook, allowing 15 to 25 minutes per pound, until juices run clear with no hint of pink when the thickest part of the thigh is pierced. Baste with brown sugar sauce during last hour of cooking time. During grilling, check coals every hour, and add a few more if necessary to maintain heat.

GRILLED CANADA GOOSE

Among the birds commonly hunted along the Northwest Coast were migrants from the North who came for the milder winter, such as the Canada goose, the snow goose, and the white-fronted goose. These wildfowl provided a tasty change from a diet of salmon; their feathered skins could be sewn into mantles, and the goose feathers twisted into cord and woven with nettles or cedar fibers to make warm flexible blankets.

Crab apples held a special place at tribal feasts. Steamed and then mashed, or combined with dried berries, they were always served with eulachon oil to important guests who ate with the large, decorated goat-horn spoons traditionally used for this dish. When a Kwakiutl chief held a formal crab-apple feast, boxes of crab apples in water and boxes of eulachon oil were displayed as wealth and then consumed to the beating of drums and the singing of newly composed feasting songs.

Traders and missionaries introduced both brown and white sugar to the Yakutat Tlingit. Brown sugar was made into cakes and later boiled down to a syrup. Lumps of brown sugar were served at feasts. In this recipe, brown sugar syrup is used to glaze the goose, which traditionally would have been spit-roasted on a green alder- or apple-wood branch held over a wood fire. Since this is impractical for most modern cooks, we suggest using a standard covered grill.

Allow goose to sit for about 15 minutes before carving.

To make the sauce: In a small saucepan, combine brown sugar and water. Cook over medium-hot heat until mixture comes to a boil. Continue stirring and cooking for 2 minutes, then remove from heat.

Serves 6

SKOKOMISH HUCKLEBERRY-GLAZED

ROAST WILD DUCK

2 mallard or pintail ducks,
dressed

2 small or medium onions,
peeled

3 cups huckleberries or
blueberries

Salt and ground pepper

¼ cup sugar

2 tablespoons water

Preheat oven to 500°F. Stuff the cavity of each duck with one quartered onion and ½ cup huckleberries. Season with salt and pepper. Reduce oven temperature to 350°F. Roast ducks on a rack, allowing 18 to 30 minutes per pound, until medium-rare or well done, depending on your taste. Baste with huckleberry sauce during last half-hour of cooking time.

To make sauce: In a saucepan, combine remaining 2 cups huckleberries, sugar, and water. Bring huckleberries to a boil, stirring constantly, and crushing berries as the sauce cooks. Boil for 2 to 3 minutes, stirring constantly, until slightly thickened.

Serves 4 to 6

Each spring, mallards, pintails, goldeneyes, and many other ducks migrate north from southern waters. Much like salmon, they return to the area where they were born to lay their eggs. Their routes take them over lakes, marshes, ponds, streams, and saltwater lagoons, allowing them to rest and feed. In the past, they came by the thousands. Where the ducks flew low, the Klallam people of Puget Sound erected poles strung with extremely fine nets some 40 feet high. At dawn or twilight, when the light was poor, flocks of ducks would fly into the nets, to be caught by hunters waiting below. The Coast Salish tied nets between trees, then startled feeding birds who became entangled in them. Netting, covered with salmon eggs, was submerged by the Makah to snare ducks feeding in the lakes and streams.

Wild duck was especially savored because it was the earliest fresh meat in the yearly food cycle. This recipe comes from Bruce Miller, the chef at the Skokomish Tribal Council in Shelton, Washington. Both huckleberries and blueberries are abundant in the Northwest, but Bruce suggests that commercially made blueberry syrup may be substituted as a glaze if you can't find fresh or frozen berries.

In a large skillet over medium heat, cook bacon until some of its fat is rendered. Add elk and brown with the bacon. Add 1 quart of water, onion, bay leaves, and salt. Cover and simmer for 1½ hours. Add potatoes, carrots, and turnip and cook 30 minutes longer. Combine remaining water with acorn meal and stir into the simmering stew.

In a bowl, combine dumpling ingredients and beat until smooth. Drop by tablespoonfuls into the simmering stew. Cover tightly and steam 12 to 15 minutes.
Serves 6

Elk, also called wapiti—a Shawnee word for "pale deer"—ranged from Vancouver Island southward and were hunted by different tribes using different methods. In winter, when snow was deep, Northern tribesmen hunted on snowshoes. A normally swift wapiti floundering in the snow was no match for men armed with yew lances who could run across the top of the snow. Hunters also drove large game animals into deep water and drowned them. The Colville, a division of the Salish on the Columbia River, hunted elk with dogs, and their kinsmen, the Stillaquamish of northwest Washington, drove them over mountain passes, much as the Plains tribes drove buffalo. After a successful hunt, the hunters often drank wapiti blood.

This recipe is typical of the Northwestern game-hunting region. Traditionally, the stew would probably have included *wapato*, a Jerusalem artichoke-like tuber, and wild parsnips. The addition of acorn dumplings is more typical of the Salish tribes east of Puget Sound and the tribes of northern California.

ELK STEW WITH ACORN DUMPLINGS

4 slices bacon, halved

1½ pounds elk or beef
    chuck steak, trimmed
    and cubed

1 quart plus ½ cup water

1¼ cups chopped onion

2 bay leaves

1 teaspoon salt (optional)

3 potatoes, peeled and
    diced

3 carrots, peeled and
    diced

1 large turnip, diced

¼ cup Acorn Meal (see
    method, page 37) or
    finely ground hazelnuts

ACORN DUMPLINGS

½ cup acorn meal or finely
    ground hazelnuts

½ cup whole wheat flour

1¾ teaspoons baking
    powder

1 egg, beaten

2 tablespoons milk

2 tablespoons vegetable
    oil

Press 5 to 6 juniper berries onto each salmon steak and season lightly with salt and pepper. Prepare grill. When coals are white-hot, sprinkle with damp wood chips. Grill steaks for 3 to 4 minutes per side until salmon flakes when probed with a fork. Serve with lemon wedges, if desired.

Serves 6

GITKSAN GRILLED SALMON STEAKS

A traditional belief among Northwest Coast Indians is that salmon are supernatural beings who live in villages beneath the sea. Every summer, disguised as fish, they come to the rivers to provide human beings with food. After a salmon is killed and eaten, it immediately reappears in its home, provided that its bones have been returned to the sea. Each tribe has a ceremony for cleaning and cooking salmon, directed—according to legend—by the Salmon People themselves. Successful hunting and fishing depend on more than the skill of the hunters. Unless treated correctly, Animal People—such as Mountain Goat, Bear, and Salmon—feel no obligation to allow their bodies to be taken.

30 to 40 dried juniper berries

6 salmon steaks, cut 1 inch thick

Salt and pepper

1½ to 2 cups alder, apple, or hickory wood chips, soaked in water

Lemon wedges (optional)

Salmon received the greatest ritual attention: In the chief's house, the first salmon was placed on a new mat and sprinkled with eagle down, its head facing upstream so that others would swim upstream too. The fish was cleaned using only fern leaves, and cut from head to tail with an ancient knife made of stone or mussel shell. Ignoring the rules would stop the salmon run. According to legend, when Chief Yaloa of the Tsimshian visited the Salmon People, his hosts were pleased with his gift of eagle down. He was treated very well; when he was hungry, a young boy, sent into the saltwater, immediately turned into a salmon. They caught him, sliced him open, and boiled him in a steaming box or grilled him above red-hot stones. After Chief Yaloa finished eating, all the bones and skin were put back into the sea and the boy returned to life.

The Gitksan Tribe used hand-held grills made from willow withes about one inch in diameter with the smaller branches still attached. The end was bent back and tied to the main stem to form a hoop large enough to support a fish steak for grilling.

1 to 3 pounds seaweed

1 to 2 dozen steamer clams

1 to 2 dozen oysters, preferably Olympia

2 pounds halibut fillets or steaks

½ to 1 teaspoon sea salt

Eulachon oil or melted butter

Lemon wedges (optional)

SKOKOMISH STEAMED SEAFOOD

The Makah, Quinault, and Quilleute, tribes of the southern coast of Puget Sound, were whaling people who built large canoes. On their expeditions they also caught halibut, huge fish that feed at the bottom of the ocean, with hook and line. The native hooks, still in use, are made of two pieces of wood lashed together with a spruce root to form a "V." A bone spike is set in one arm of the V, and the other arm, which holds the line, is carved to represent a spirit helper, usually an animal or bird. The line, a rope of spruce root or kelp, is weighted with a heavy stone so that the hook, baited with squid, floats a few feet above the ocean floor. Attached at the upper end is a buoy of carved cedar, representing a sea bird. When this float bobs, the fisherman pulls up his line, and if he has caught a halibut, he kills it with a beautifully carved club.

The anthropologist Franz Boas recorded many incantations and prayers used by native fishermen when catching halibut, which they called by colorful names. Some were recited to the hook, which they called "younger brother": "Go down to halibut land and fight"; when there was a bite, "Hold on, younger brother." And some to the fish. When stunning a fish with a club: "Go and tell your father, your mother, your uncle, your aunt, your eldest and youngest brothers, that you had good luck because you came to this, my fishing canoe, you Old Woman, Flabby-Skin-in-the-Mouth, Born-to-be-Given."

The use of seaweed for steaming fish is traditional. The Salish dig a large firepit or *imu* and lay stones at the bottom. A wood fire, started on top of the stones, burns down to glowing coals. When all the stones are intensely hot, the coals are raked aside. Pieces of green sand-free seaweed are laid on top of the rocks; then chunks of halibut, wrapped in ferns or maple leaves, are placed on the seaweed and covered with additional seaweed. Finally, the *imu* is covered with gravel. Within an hour, the delicious results of steaming are ready. A similar effect can be achieved in a modern kitchen using this recipe, given to us by Bruce Miller—a talented and knowledgeable Skokomish chef—who with the help of his family organizes and caters traditional Native American feasts for up to fifteen hundred people.

To a large steamer pot or deep, covered roasting pan with rack, add enough water for steaming. Heat until boiling. Place a layer of seaweed on the rack. Put clams and oysters on the seaweed. Add another layer of seaweed, followed by the fish. Cover with seaweed. Sprinkle lightly with sea salt. Cover and steam for 10 to 15 minutes, until fish flakes easily and clams and oysters have opened. Serve with Eulachon oil or butter and lemon wedges.
Serves 4 to 6

RAW SALMON

1 very fresh, raw salmon fillet (about 1½ pounds)
Warm eulachon oil or melted butter (optional)
Lemon wedges (optional)

Salmon-catching methods were adapted to the nature of the waters in which they were found. In foaming rapids, men on shore held nets with 20-foot handles, as they do today, dipping salmon while standing on water-sprayed rocks or atop slippery wooden platforms mounted on rocks that projected over the turbulent waters. In shallow rapids, they harpooned salmon through the rough waters, or threw harpoons at the leaping salmon. In deep, wide rivers, men used canoes to sweep the salmon into nets that were several hundred feet long.

Although the Tlingit, Haida, and Tsimshian generally cooked their food, the roe of salmon and herring were often eaten raw, as was the fresh salmon caught at the first run.

Ed Sarabia, who works with the United States Environmental Protection Agency in Hartford, Connecticut, is a member of the Tlingit tribe and was born in Juneau, Alaska. Ed recalls that when he was growing up, the cheeks of freshly caught raw salmon were a very special delicacy among his people.

With a very sharp knife, slice fillet on a slight angle into ⅓-inch-thick pieces. If desired, dip in warm oil and sprinkle with lemon juice.
Serves 6 as an appetizer

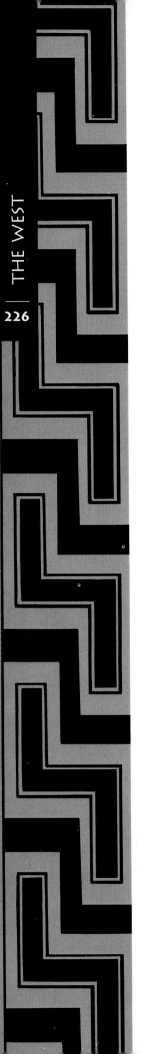

Smoked salmon was an essential part of the diet of the Northwest Coast cultures. Because of the predictability of salmon runs from spring through fall, the possibility of huge catches, and the Indians' techniques for preservation, dried smoked salmon became a year-round staple.

Drying and smoking salmon for winter was women's work. Slow-burning alder fires, which produced the best smoke, were built along beaches, in smokehouses, and often in native dwellings. The fish were cut open, and smooth round cedar "hanging sticks," inserted through a series of slits made on opposite sides of the fish, were used to spread the fish apart. The salmon hung, like crimson shields, on drying racks five to nine feet above the fire, which was adjusted to smoke freely yet give minimal heat. Every day or two, the fish were rubbed and squeezed to break the fibers and to allow air to penetrate the flesh. Careful attention was necessary and rain would mean a rush to cover them all.

The amount of smoking time depends on the results desired. Hard-smoked and fully dried fish require a week or more, and keep indefinitely. By contrast, this recipe is for a delicately flavored, soft-smoked salmon. It doesn't keep (unless it is frozen), so must be enjoyed immediately.

½ cup coarse (kosher) salt

½ cup brown sugar

1½ teaspoons ground ginger (optional)

1 teaspoon coarsely ground black pepper (optional)

1 salmon fillet, about 1½ pounds

1 to 2 cups alder, apple, or hickory wood chips, soaked in water for at least ½ hour

In a mixing bowl, combine salt, sugar, ginger, and pepper. Coat fillet with this seasoning mix. Wrap well or place in a plastic bag and refrigerate for at least 2 hours. Wash salt from the fillet and rinse well. Let salmon air-dry thoroughly for 1 to 2 hours, until a sheen appears on the fish. To dry in the open air, suspend the fish from the limb of a tree or place it on a rack so that air can circulate around it. To dry indoors, suspend in front of a fan.

ALDER-SMOKED SALMON

Proceed to smoking by preparing the grill. Bank a generous amount of medium-hot coals around a drip pan. Sprinkle wood chips on the coals. Place the fish over drip pan. Cover grill and smoke until the fish flakes easily, about ¾ hour. Serves 6 as an appetizer

**2 to 3 dozen butter clams
or 4 dozen steamer
clams, shucked**

**8 to 10 wooden skewers,
soaked in water
Eulachon oil, sardine oil,
or melted butter**

**½ cup to 1 cup alder, apple,
or hickory wood chips,
soaked in water for at
least ½ hour**

Clams, mussels, abalone, and crabs have always provided variety to the coastal diet. Women gathered them at low tide, much as they do today. Implements, too, have remained the same—pointed digging sticks to pry up clams and cockles and overturn crabs, and canes for scrambling over rocks for chitons and seaweed. Water buckets and gunny sacks have replaced traditional open-weave baskets, lightening the load of the gatherer.

Giant horse clams require an extra-long and hard digging stick, with a scoop at the end, so the clams can be dislodged from under several feet of sand. A single clam can make a whole chowder. Butter clams, lying close to shore just inches down, are more easily gathered. The Salish enjoyed them steamed, and also smoked them for winter soups.

BARBECUED CLAMS

Thread 4 to 6 clams on each skewer. Brush with oil. Prepare barbecue grill. Sprinkle wood chips over hot coals. Grill clams for 3 to 8 minutes, depending on their size. Turn and baste once with oil. Serve with additional oil for dipping.
Serves 4 to 6

Few foods spoil more rapidly than fresh clams. Smoking clams is an effective way to preserve them. The Indians strung smoked clams on cedar-bark fibers to dry further. These clam "necklaces" were traded for baskets with inland tribes, who hungered for seafood, and were also worn by babies as a kind of teething ring. Fresh clams, skewered on spruce twigs, were barbecued over a fire.

Traditionally the clams in this recipe would be grilled as described above and then dipped in eulachon oil. The Skokomish chef Bruce Miller tells us that, today, those who favor a slightly milder dipping sauce use the oil from canned sardines or melted butter.

1 dozen small oysters
(preferably Olympia),
shucked

4 cups mashed potatoes or
Jerusalem artichokes

1 egg

⅔ cup thinly sliced green
onions

2 tablespoons chopped
fresh dill weed or 1½
teaspoons dried

2 teaspoons salt, or to
taste

½ teaspoon ground pepper
(optional)

2 tablespoons unbleached
flour

About ¼ cup vegetable
oil or bacon drippings,
for frying

OLYMPIA OYSTER-POTATO CAKES

Tiny Olympia oysters, with their distinctive, slightly coppery tang, were once abundant in the waters of Puget Sound and along the Northwest Coast. Unfortunately, these bivalves, whose rosy violet-tinged inner shells resemble a Pacific sunset, are rare today. The blander Pacific oyster, grown locally from Japanese seed, is more common.

Native Americans along the Northwest Coast prepare oysters in many ways. They are eaten raw, smoked on the half shell, and also used in soups, fritters, and cakes, like those in this recipe.

Preheat oven to 275°F. Drain oysters and reserve. In a mixing bowl, combine potatoes with egg, green onions, dill, and salt and pepper. With lightly floured hands, form potato mixture into patties. Place an oyster in the middle of each patty and enclose it completely with potato. In a large skillet, heat 2 tablespoons of oil.

Add the cakes 2 to 3 at a time and fry over medium heat until golden brown on both sides, 6 to 8 minutes. Remove to a baking sheet and keep warm in the oven until all are cooked. Add more oil as needed during frying.
Serves 4 to 6

1 quart fresh raspberries

½ cup honey

Puree berries with honey until smooth. Chill well and serve.
Serves 4 to 6

WHIPPED RASPBERRIES AND HONEY

Berry-gathering was a pleasureful activity for Northwest Coast women who had worked hard preparing and preserving freshly caught fish and game. In early spring, berries provided both essential vitamins and a change of taste, but most enjoyable was the opportunity for women and girls to arrange gathering parties for themselves. Occasionally camping excursions were planned during which women from different villages would share each other's company, exchanging news as they worked in the berry patches. Some did the picking, others looked after the children. When women went through the woods to reach the berries, they kept close together for fear of evil forest spirits, and called out often to scare off bears who might also be after berries.

Fresh raspberries were sometimes mixed with salmon eggs and eulachon oil. A feast dish was made of mixed dried berries beaten with eulachon oil and snow. Soapberries whipped to a froth and combined with eulachon oil, sometimes called "Indian ice cream," were an eagerly anticipated treat. Today, mothers whip berries with honey or sugar as a special dessert for their children.

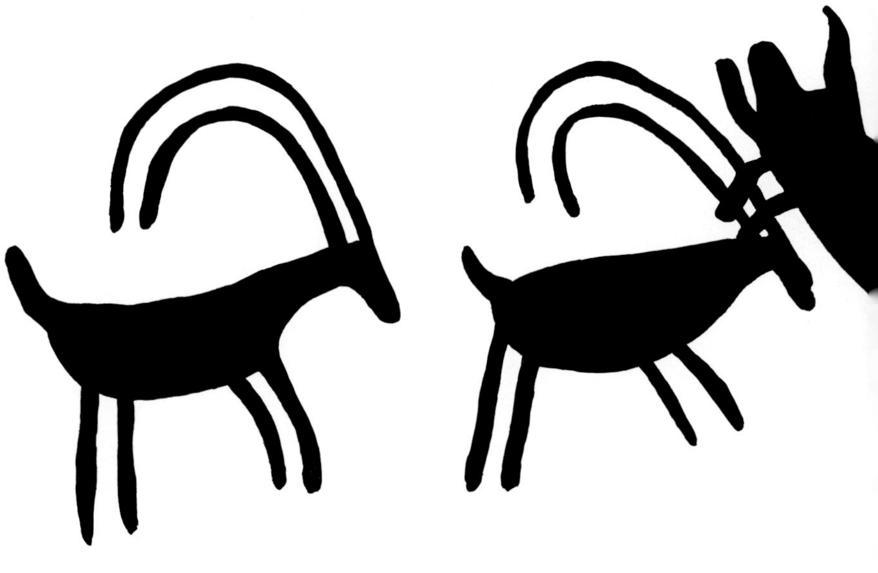

When large amounts of berries were in season, whole families might go on berry-picking expeditions in canoes. The young men would be busy all day carrying back filled baskets. Berry-pickers often used three baskets of graduated sizes. They were four-sided, nested, and held on the back by a "tump-line" across the forehead. When women began picking, the smallest basket was hung in front from their belts, and the mid-size and the largest, or "swallowing," baskets were placed on the ground, to be filled from the heaping small baskets. Women could carry two full baskets back, one on either side, with the smallest one hanging over the chest.

Fresh wild strawberries were often pounded or mashed into a puree or poached in honey syrup. Traditionally, the Tlingit cooked strawberries to a hardened paste, formed it into small cakes, and wrapped the cakes in skunk cabbage leaves to dry. One cake poached in warm water could produce "a plate full of strawberries," most delicious with honey on a gray, rainy winter's day.

STRAWBERRIES POACHED IN HONEY SYRUP

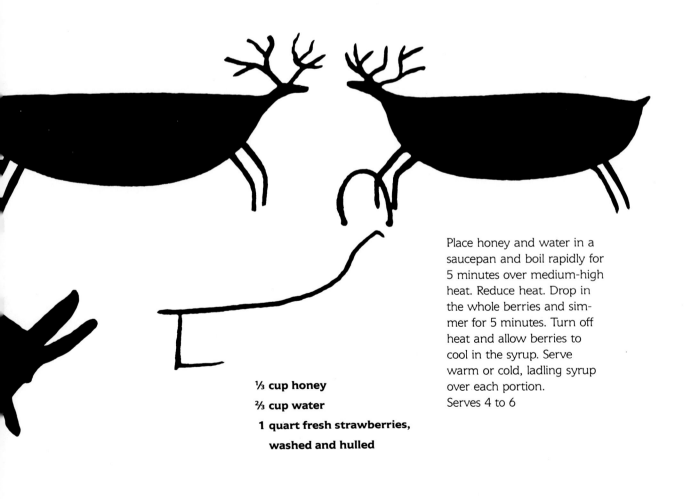

Place honey and water in a saucepan and boil rapidly for 5 minutes over medium-high heat. Reduce heat. Drop in the whole berries and simmer for 5 minutes. Turn off heat and allow berries to cool in the syrup. Serve warm or cold, ladling syrup over each portion.
Serves 4 to 6

⅓ cup honey

⅔ cup water

1 quart fresh strawberries, washed and hulled

2 cups huckleberries or
blueberries
3 cups unbleached flour
½ cup sugar
1¼ teaspoons baking
powder
3 eggs
½ cup water
Oil, for deep-frying

HUCKLEBERRY FRITTERS

Large supplies of berries were gathered and preserved by all Northwestern tribes. Berry-picking grounds were clan-owned, and outsiders would have to ask permission to pick there.

Four varieties of huckleberries were especially enjoyed: coastal, tall blue forest, black mountain, and evergreen. To gather the tiny black coastal huckleberry, Lummi women used wooden combs to sweep both leaves and berries into their baskets. At home, the contents were rolled down the wetted surface of a tilted cedar plank, allowing the berries to collect in waiting baskets while the leaves stuck to the wet plank. Today, berries are boiled with sugar and put up in mason jars, or stored raw, covered with sugar. This latter preparation makes excellent fritters.

Wash berries and allow to drain. Sift dry ingredients together into a mixing bowl. Beat eggs with water until foamy. Mix quickly into dry ingredients. Fold in berries. Heat oil or shortening in deep heavy skillet to 350°F. on a deep-frying thermometer or until a bread cube dropped in the oil turns golden brown in 1 minute.

Drop batter by tablespoonfuls into the hot oil. Turn fritters frequently so that they brown to a deep golden color on all sides. Drain on paper towels and serve hot. Makes 2 dozen

Cranberry and Huckleberry Fritters

The dough used for making the fritters in this recipe is a sweetened version of the basic fry bread dough popular with Native Americans in all regions. The Northwestern idea of forming the dough around a firm berry is interesting and fun. If eaten immediately, they are delicious.

¾ cup fresh cranberries

1½ cups unbleached flour

¾ cup granulated sugar

1 tablespoon baking powder

¼ teaspoon salt

½ cup plus 1 tablespoon milk

¼ cup dark brown sugar

Oil, for deep-frying

Confectioners' sugar (optional)

CRANBERRY FRITTERS

Wash cranberries and dry on paper towels. Sift dry ingredients together and mix in milk gradually to form a stiff dough. With well-floured hands, pinch off 1 teaspoon of dough and make an indentation. Sprinkle a little brown sugar in the indentation and place a cranberry in the center. Roll dough around the berry. Balls should be about the size of a large marble. Heat oil in a deep, heavy kettle until the temperature reaches 375°F. on a deep-frying thermometer or until a bread cube turns golden brown in 30 to 40 seconds. Drop fritter balls into the hot fat and fry, turning, until they are deep golden brown on all sides. Drain on paper towels. If desired, shake confectioners' sugar over the fritters just before serving.

Makes 3 dozen

Berries, both fresh and dried, were important in the diet of the Northwestern tribes. According to the Skokomish chef Bruce Miller, the wild cranberry, about a quarter of the size of those sold commercially, is only one of the many varieties of berries available in the Northwest.

Traditionally, fresh berries were cooked by placing alternating layers of berries and heated stones in a special cedar cooking box or a tightly woven basket. After the stones were removed, the cooked berries—depending on the variety and the desired use—were either left to sit and thicken or were thickened more quickly by an addition of dried powdered berries or powdered skunk cabbage leaves. Thickened berries were formed into cakes and placed on wooden drying racks lined with skunk cabbage leaves. After drying over a hot alder-wood fire, the finished cakes were stacked and tied with soft shredded cedar bark and stored in a warm, dry place for future use.

Jam- and jelly-making as we know them today date back only to as far as European contact. Since berries are so abundant in this region, however, both are now a popular way to preserve the berry harvest.

CRANBERRY JELLY

Combine berries and water in a heavy saucepan. Bring the cranberries to a boil over high heat. Reduce heat to low and simmer until all the berries are soft, 10 to 15 minutes. Line a large colander or strainer with 2 thicknesses of cheesecloth and suspend over a large pot. Pour cranberries and cooking water into the cheesecloth-lined colander. Allow to drain without mashing the berries or squeezing the cheesecloth for 10 to 12 hours. Discard berries and cheesecloth. Add sugar to the cranberry juice and cook over medium-high heat for 15 to 20 minutes. Pour into sterilized jelly jars and seal with paraffin, if desired.
Makes 3 to 3½ cups

4 cups cranberries

4 cups water

5 cups sugar

APPENDIX

ACORNS

Native Americans in several regions ate acorns. Among the California tribes, they were an important dietary staple. A few varieties of "sweet acorns," such as those of the white oak, may be eaten raw, but most acorns must be leached to remove their bitter tannin.

Methods for leaching acorns vary regionally. The easiest one we have found is to place hulled acorns in a large saucepan with water to cover and bring them to a boil. Boil for thirty minutes, drain, and add fresh water. Repeat this process at least three times, or until the water is a very light tea color and the bitter taste of the acorns is gone. Dry the leached nut meats in the sun or in a slow oven (150°F.) When dried, they may be ground into flour or chopped into a coarser meal. Acorn flour or meal is blended with wheat flour to make breads and biscuits, and acorn meal is used to make a nourishing gruel or porridge.

CAMAS

Camas bulbs were one of the principal foods of the Shoshone, Bannock, and Flathead tribes of the Plateau region. Sometimes called wild hyacinth or prairie apple, the camas is botanically related to the hyacinth. The bulbs have a high sugar content and are prepared by pit roasting or by flattening into cakes and sun-drying for storage. The taste of roasted camas has been described as being very sweet and resembling vanilla. In modern recipes, dried dates are sometimes used as a substitute. Dried camas has been compared in flavor to a sweet onion.

Note: It is important to harvest camas only when it is in bloom. The edible camas has blue blossoms, whereas the poisonous Death Camas—often found growing in the same locations—has white blossoms.

CHILIES

Chilies *(capsicum),* like potatoes and tomatoes, are members of the Deadly Nightshade family. More than thirty varieties are grown worldwide. They are low in calories and high in vitamins A and C.

Archeological finds indicate that chilies have been cultivated in South and Central America since about 7000 B.C. Columbus found them growing in the West Indies, and European traders carried them to Africa and Asia, where they have become an important element in several cuisines.

Chilies have been used in the native cooking of the Southwest since the sixteenth century, when they were introduced from Mexico by the Spaniards.

The important southwestern chili varieties are listed below, beginning with the milder ones and ending with the hottest:

New Mexico Long Green or Red Chilies, also called **Anaheim Chilies** These long, slightly twisted chilies vary in color from green to red and in heat from mild to medium-hot. They are used fresh and may also be dried and ground. These are the chilies that, in their dried state, are most often used to make the large chili strings and wreaths called *ristras* in the Southwest.

Poblanos These mild but flavorful chilies are eaten green. They have smooth, shiny skin and—except for their pointed tips—resemble small, slightly flattened green bell peppers. They are ideal for stuffing and are also often cut into thin strips (*rajas*) or chopped and added to other dishes. When dried, poblanos are usually called *chiles anchos,* although sometimes they are called *pisados* in Texas and *pasillas* in California.

Jalapeños Jalapeños are the most widely eaten fresh hot chilies in the United States. They vary in color from green to red. Jalapeños are often roasted and peeled, but may also be eaten raw or pickled (*en escabeche*). When they are dried and smoked, they are called "*chiles chipotles.*"

Serranos Smaller, hotter, and a bit more pointed than jalapeños, these green to red chilies are often used in fresh salsas and may also be packed in oil or pickled.

Pequin These green to red chilies are a typical ingredient of northern New Mexican cooking. They are about three inches long, slender, and hot. They may be used fresh or dried and ground.

Chiltepines These tiny red chilies grow wild in the canyons of southern Arizona and northern Mexico. They are very hot. One or two added to a stew is usually enough to give it punch.

HANDLING CHILIES

When handling hot chilies, it is prudent to wear rubber gloves and keep your hands away from your eyes. Capsaicin, the source of heat in chilies, is concentrated in the ribs and the seeds. To cut down on their heat, slit chilies with the tip of a small, sharp knife and carefully shave off ribs and discard seeds.

PEELING CHILIES

Green chilies are often roasted and peeled before being added to a dish. This procedure improves both flavor and digestibility. To peel, make a small slit near the stem end of chilies. Preheat oven to 400°F. Spread chilies on a baking sheet and roast, turning often, until all sides are black and blistered. Small amounts of chilies may also be roasted directly over the flame of a gas stove or placed on the grill over hot coals. Spread a damp towel over roasted chilies and allow to cool. Carefully pull and scrape skin from cooled chilies.

FREEZING CHILIES

For best results, place cooled, blistered, but unpeeled chilies in a plastic container and freeze for up to one year. Defrost enough to separate and slip off skins. Chopped chilies may also be frozen for up to six months.

CORN OR MAIZE

Corn is probably the most important Native American food. There are five basic varieties of native Indian corn and many hybrids. The fresh corn we eat today is a mature, hybridized version of sweet corn, but up until the 1920s corn on the cob was "green corn," the immature ears of several varieties. There are several products made from corn that are used in Native American cooking, including:

Atole Finely ground, toasted blue cornmeal. The Hopi combine it with powdered milk, sugar, and water to make a traditional drink of the same name.

Chicos Dried, unhulled, whole corn kernels that can be reconstituted by soaking in water and boiling until tender.

Grits Dried hominy that has been ground into a coarse meal. Used to make a porridge eaten for breakfast or as a side dish.

Hominy An Anglicized Algonquian term for fresh or dried corn kernels that have been soaked or boiled with hardwood ashes, unslaked lime, or caustic soda to remove their tough outer hulls. Hominy may be rinsed well and cooked or ground directly after this process or dried again to be stored until needed. In the Southwest, it is called posole.

Masa Meal freshly made from grinding wet hominy. Used to make tortillas and tamales.

Masa Harina Masa that has been dried.

Parched Corn Whole corn kernels that have been toasted or roasted. Parched corn is reconstituted by soaking in water and boiling until tender.

CULINARY ASHES

Early Native Americans somehow knew that adding wood ash to corn dishes raised their mineral content and increased the amount of available protein. The alkaline in the ashes acts as a food supplement to balance the amino acids in which corn is deficient and makes it a well-balanced, life-sustaining food. Culinary ashes are made by burning hardwood, bushes, or herbs until they turn to ash. In the Southeast, Creek and Seminole cooks use hickory. In the Southwest, the Navajo use juniper branches and the Hopi favor the ash made from the chamisa bush. Ashes were also used as a leavening agent in corn breads and as a seasoning in other dishes. Today, baking soda is sometimes substituted for ashes.

EULACHON OR CANDLEFISH OIL

Eulachon, sometimes called hooligan fish or candlefish, are members of the smelt family. They are so rich in oil that when threaded with a wick, they can be used as candles. The oil is also used as a condiment for salmon and as an ingredient in desserts made from berries. Eulachon oil is still available in limited quantities locally in the Northwest, although many people today prefer the slightly milder taste of the oil from canned sardines.

NATIVE PERSIMMONS

Native American persimmons grow wild throughout the Southeast. The fruit is walnut-size, distinctive in flavor, and usually only available regionally. Like Hachiya persimmons from Japan, native persimmons should only be eaten when ripe.

SORGHUM MOLASSES

Sorghum molasses is a bit stronger and not quite as sweet as cane molasses, but they may be used interchangeably in most recipes.

MAIL ORDER SOURCES

CANNED PERSIMMON PUREE

Dymple's Delight Canned Persimmons
Route 4, Box 53
Mitchell, Indiana 47446
Tel. (812) 849-3487

SORGHUM MOLASSES

Bobby Bryan's Sorghum Molasses
7472 Wallace Lane
Wallace, Mississippi 38680
Tel. (601) 781-3434

BEANS, CHILI, AND CORN PRODUCTS

The Chili Shop Inc.
109 East Water Street
Santa Fe, New Mexico 87501
Tel. (505) 983-6080

Los Chileros de Nuevo Mexico
P.O. Box 6215
Santa Fe, New Mexico 87502
Tel. (505) 471-6967

Native Seeds/Search
2509 N. Cambel Avenue #325
Tucson, Arizona 85719

ALDER-SMOKED SALMON AND OYSTERS

Eddie Bauer Inc.
Tel. (800) 426-8020

GAME

Lucky Star Ranch
RR #1 Box 273
Chaumont, New York 13622
Tel. (607) 836-4766

The Game Exchange
107 Quint Street
San Francisco, California 94124
Tel. (415) 282-7878 or (800) 426-3872

BIBLIOGRAPHY

GENERAL

Driver, Harold E. *Indians of North America*. Chicago: University of Chicago Press, 1969.

Eagle Walking Turtle. *Indian America*. Santa Fe, NM: John Muir Publications, 1989.

Fussell, Betty. *I Hear America Cooking*. New York: Viking Press, 1986.

Grant, Bruce. *Concise Encyclopedia of the American Indian*. New York: Bonanza Books, 1989.

Hays, Wilma, and R. Vernon. *Foods the Indians Gave Us*. New York: Ives Washburn, Inc., 1973.

Houston, Alice Watson. *The American Heritage Book of Fish Cookery*. New York: American Heritage Publishing Company, 1980.

Kavasch, Barrie. *Native Harvests*. New York: Random House, 1979.

Kimball, Yeffe, and Jean Anderson. *The Art of American Indian Cooking*. Garden City, NY: Doubleday & Co., 1965.

Reader's Digest. *America's Fascinating Indian Heritage*. Pleasantville, NY: Readers Digest Association, 1978.

Sokolov, Raymond. *Fading Feast*. New York: Farrar, Straus, & Giroux, 1981.

Stoutenburgh, John, Jr. *Dictionary of the American Indian*. New York: Bonanza Books, 1960.

Weatherford, Jack. *Indian Givers*. New York: Crown Publishers, 1988.

Williamson, Darcy, and Lisa Railsback. *Cooking with Spirit, North American Indian Food and Fact*. Bend, OR: Maverick Publications, 1988.

SOUTHEASTERN COAST AND WOODLANDS

Bumgarner, Rubye Alley. *Sunset Farms*. Franklin, NC: Macon Graphics, 1980.

Buikstra, Jane E. "The Lower Illinois River Region: A Prehistoric Context for the Study of Ancient Diet and Health" *Paleopathology at the Origins of Agriculture*, Mark Nathan Cohen and George J. Armelagos, eds. New York: Academic Press, 1984.

Harriot, Thomas. *A Brief and True Report of the New Found Land of Virginia: The Complete 1590 Theodor de Bry Edition*. New York: Dover Publications, 1970.

Harris, Gladiola B. *Old Trace Cooking*. Memphis, TN: Riverside Press, 1988.

Lewis, H. Larson. *Aboriginal Subsistence Technology on the Southeastern Coastal Plain During the Late Prehistoric Period*. Gainesville: University Presses of Florida, 1980.

Marriott, Alice, and Carol K. Rachlin. *American Indian Mythology*. New York: New American Library, 1968.

Mooney, James. *Myths of the Cherokee*, Nineteenth Annual Report of the Bureau of American Ethnology, reprinted Nashville. Nashville, TN: Charles and Randy Elder, 1982.

Whisler, Frances Lambert. *Indian Cookin*. Chattanooga, TN: Nowega Press, 1973.

NORTHEASTERN COAST AND WOODLANDS

Aeisberger, David. *David Aeisberger's History of the North American Indians*, Archer Butler Hulbert and William Nathaniel Schwarze, eds. Columbus: Ohio State Archaeological and Historical Society, 1910.

Bruchac, Joseph. *The Faithful Hunter: Abnaki Stories*. Greenfield Center, NY: Greenfield Review Press, 1988.

Morgan, Henry Lewis. *League of the Iroquois*. New York: Corinth Books, 1962.

Richard, Asa Yarnell. *Aboriginal Relationships Between Culture and Plant Life in the Upper Great Lakes Region*. Anthropological Papers, Museum of Anthropology, University of Michigan, No. 23. Ann Arbor: University of Michigan, 1964.

Tantaquidgeon, Gladys. *Folk Medicine of the Delaware and Related Algonkian Indians*, Anthropological Series Number 3.

Harrisburg, PA: Commonwealth of Pennsylvania, Pennsylvania Historical and Museum Commission, 1972.

Thomas, Vennum. *Wild Rice and the Ojibay People*. St. Paul: Minnesota Historical Society Press, 1988.

GREAT PLAINS

Black Elk, Wallace, and William S. Lyon. *Black Elk, the Sacred Ways of a Lakota*. San Francisco: Harper & Row, 1990.

Densmore, Frances. *How Indians Use Wild Plants for Food, Medicine & Crafts*. New York: Dover Publications, 1974.

Gilmore, Melvin R. *Uses of Plants by the Indians of the Missouri River Region*. Lincoln, NE: University of Nebraska Press, 1977.

Hungry Wolf, Beverly. *The Ways of My Grandmothers*. New York: William Morrow and Company, 1980.

McPherson, John and Geri. *Primitive Wilderness Cooking Methods*. Manhattan, KS: Ag Press, 1990.

Walker, Herb. *Indian Cookin*. Amarillo, TX: Baxter Lane Co., 1977.

Wilson, Gilbert L. *Buffalo Bird Woman's Garden*. St. Paul: Minnesota Historical Society Press, 1987.

SOUTHWEST

Basso, K.H., and M.E. Opler, eds., "Apachean Culture, History, and Ethnology," Anthropological Papers of the University of Arizona Press, 21. Tucson, AZ: University of Arizona Press, 1971.

Brugge, E. D., *A History of the Chaco Navajos*, Reports of the Chaco Center, no. 4, Division of Chaco Research, National Park Service. Albuquerque, NM: National Park Service, 1980.

Cushing, F. H., *Zuni Breadstuffs, Indian Notes and Monographs* VIII. New York: Heye Foundation, 1920.

deBenitez, A. M., *Prehispanic Cooking*. Mexico: Klaus Thiele, 1974.

Dyk, Walter, *Son of Old Man Hat*. Lincoln, NE: University of Nebraska Press, 1967.

Evers, L., ed., "Between Sacred Mountains." Tucson, AZ: University of Arizona Press, 1984.

Franciscan Fathers, *An Ethnographic Dictionary of the Navajo Language*. Saint Michael's, AZ: Saint Michael's Press, 1968. Reprint.

Hesse, Zora. *Southwestern Indian Recipe Book*. Palmer Lake, CO: Filter Press, 1973.

Hughes, Phyllis. *Recipes from the Pueblos of the American Southwest*. Santa Fe, NM: Museum of New Mexico Press, 1984.

Keegan, Marcia. *Southwest Indian Cookbook*. Weehawken, NJ: Clear Light Publications, 1977.

Kennedy, Diana. *The Tortilla Book*. New York: Harper and Row, 1975.

Kluckhohn, C., and D. Leighton. *The Navajo*. New York: Doubleday and Co., 1962.

Lister, Robert H. and Florence C. *Those Who Came Before*. Tucson, AZ: University of Arizona Press, 1983.

Luckert, Karl W., *The Navajo Hunter Tradition*. Tucson, AZ: University of Arizona Press, 1975.

Niethammer, Carolyn. *American Indian Food and Lore*. New York: Collier Books, Macmillan Publishing Co., 1974.

Parsons. E.C., *Pueblo Indian Religion*, Vol. I. Chicago: University of Chicago Press, 1939. Midway reprint, 1974.

Reichard, Gladys A. *Navajo Religion*. Bollingen Series XVIII (1950), 2nd ed., Princeton: Princeton University Press, 1970.

Roberts, J. M., *Three Navajo Households*. Papers of the Peabody Museum of American Archeology and Ethnology XL (1951), Krauss reprint, 1973.

Roessel Jr., R.A., *Dinetah, Navajo History*, Vol. II. Rough Rock, AZ: Navajo Curriculum Center, 1983.

Russell, F., *The Pima Indians* Twenty-Sixth Annual Report of the Bureau of American Ethnology, 1904–1905, Smithsonian Institution, Washington, DC (1908). Tucson: University of Arizona Press, reprint 1975.

Scully, Vincent. *Pueblo: Mountain, Village, Dance*. New York: Viking Press, 1975.

Spicer, E. H. *Cycles of Conquest*. Tucson: University of Arizona Press, 1972.

Tiger Kavena, Juanita. *Hopi Cookery*. Tucson: University of Arizona Press, 1987.

Underhill, Ruth. *Here Come the Navajo*. Washington, DC: U.S. Department of the Interior, Bureau of Indian Affairs, 1953.

———. *The Papago and Pima Indians of Arizona*. Palmer Lake, CO: Filter Press, 1979.

———. *People of the Crimson Evening*. Washington, DC: U.S. Department of the Interior, Bureau of Indian Affairs, 1951.

———. *Workday Life of the Pueblo*. Washington, DC: U.S. Department of the Interior, Bureau of Indian Affairs, 1954.

Waters, R., *Book of the Hopi*. New York: Viking Press, 1963.

Yazzie E., *Navajo History*. Vol. I, Navajo Curriculum Center, Chinle, AZ: Rough Neck Demonstration School, 1971.

WEST

Barrett, S. A., and E. W. Gifford. "Indian Life of the Yosemite Region," Milwaukee, WI: Bulletins of the Milwaukee Public Museum 2, 1933.

Batdorf, C. *Northwest Native Harvest*. Blaine, WA: Hancock House Publishers, 1990.

Boas, F. *Ethnology of the Kwakiutl*. Thirty-Fifth Annual Report of the Bureau of American Ethnology, 1913–1914. Washington, DC: Smithsonian Institution, 1921.

de Laguna, F. *Under Mount Saint Elias: The History and Culture of the Yakutat Tlingit*. Smithsonian Contributions to Anthropology 7, Pt.1, 1972.

Gunther, E. *Indian Life on the Northwest Coast*. Chicago: University of Chicago Press, 1972.

Kirk, Ruth. *Tradition and Change on the Northwest Coast*. Seattle: University of Washington Press, 1986.

Krause, Aurel. *The Tlinget Indians*. Seattle: University of Seattle Press, 1885.

McMillan, A. D. *Native Peoples and Cultures of Canada*, Vancouver, BC: Douglas and McIntyre, 1988.

Spencer, Robert F., Jesse D. Jennings, et al. *The Native Americans*. New York: Harper and Row, 1965.

Underhill, Ruth. *Indians of the Pacific Northwest*. Washington, DC: Bureau of Indian Affairs, 1945.

CONVERSIONS

LIQUID MEASURES

FLUID OUNCES	U.S. MEASURES	IMPERIAL MEASURES	MILLILITERS
	1 TSP	1 TSP	5
¼	2 TSP	1 DESSERT SPOON	7
½	1 TBS	1 TBS	15
1	2 TBS	2 TBS	28
2	¼ CUP	4 TBS	56
4	½ CUP OR ¼ PINT		110
5		¼ PINT OR 1 GILL	140
6	¾ CUP		170
8	1 CUP OR ½ PINT		225
9			250, ¼ LITER
10	1¼ CUPS	½ PINT	280
12	1½ CUPS OR ¾ PINT		240
15		¾ PINT	420
16	2 CUPS OR 1 PINT		450
18	2¼ CUPS		500, ½ LITER
20	2½ CUPS	1 PINT	560
24	3 CUPS OR 1½ PINTS		675
25		1¼ PINTS	700
27	3½ CUPS		750
30	3¾ CUPS	1½ PINTS	840
32	4 CUPS OR 2 PINTS OR 1 QUART		900
35		1¼ PINTS	980
36	4½ CUPS		1000, 1 LITER

SOLID MEASURES

U.S. AND IMPERIAL MEASURES OUNCES	POUNDS	METRIC MEASURES GRAMS	KILOS
1		28	
2		56	
3½		100	
4	¼	112	
5		140	
6		168	
8	½	225	
9		250	¼
12	¾	340	
16	1	450	
18		500	½
20	1¼	560	
24	1½	675	
27		750	¾
28	1¾	780	
32	2	900	
36	2¼	1000	1
40	2½	1100	
48	3	1350	
54		1500	1½

OVEN TEMPERATURE EQUIVALENTS

FAHRENHEIT	GAS MARK	CELSIUS	HEAT OF OVEN
225	¼	107	VERY COOL
250	½	121	VERY COOL
275	1	135	COOL
300	2	148	COOL
325	3	163	MODERATE
350	4	177	MODERATE
375	5	190	FAIRLY HOT
400	6	204	FAIRLY HOT
425	7	218	HOT
450	8	232	VERY HOT
475	9	246	VERY HOT

PHOTOGRAPHIC PROP CREDITS

Page 2: Rug and kachina, collection of Harriet and Seymour Koenig.

Page 6: Bear Society shield, courtesy Prairie's Edge, Santa Fe, New Mexico.

Page 31: Cherokee basket, courtesy The Common Ground, New York.

Page 34: Apache basket and prehistoric stone pipe, courtesy The Common Ground, New York.

Page 43: Seminole skirt, courtesy The Common Ground, New York.

Page 57: Arrows courtesy Friedman Gallery, Westport, Connecticut; cutting board courtesy Pat Guthman Antiques, Southport, Connecticut.

Page 64: Bean pot courtesy Canyon Road, New Canaan, Connecticut; wood ladle courtesy Friedman Gallery, Westport, Connecticut; cow horn spoon with quillwork, c. 1880, courtesy Historic North American Indian Art, New York.

Page 69: Seneca Iroquois mask, c. 1890–1910, courtesy Historic North American Indian Art, New York; 18th-century Northeastern burl bowl and effigy spoon, courtesy Pat Guthman Antiques, Southport, Connecticut.

Page 77: Ojibway birchbark basket, courtesy Canyon Road, New Canaan, Connecticut; Iroquois beaded purse, c. 1880, courtesy Historic North American Indian Art, New York; Iroquois flint fish hook, excavated in New York State, courtesy Guthman Americana, Westport, Connecticut.

Page 80: Iroquois moccasin, c. 1870, courtesy Historic North American Indian Art, New York; wooden bowl, courtesy Canyon Road, New Canaan, Connecticut.

Page 83: 19th-century Winnebago beaded sash, courtesy Historic North American Indian Art, New York.

Page 91: Wooden ladle and wooden spoon, courtesy Guthman Americana, Westport, Connecticut; Algonquian birchbark box, cour-

tesy Historic North American Indian Art, New York.

Page 94: Penobscot birchbark container and Ojibway birchbark container with quillwork, courtesy Historic American Indian Art, New York.

Page 105: Thunderbird dance stick, courtesy Prairie's Edge, Santa Fe, New Mexico.

Page 108: Sioux medicine cup made of cow horn, courtesy Historic North American Indian Art, New York.

Page 112: Ghost Dance shirt and drum and drumstick, courtesy Prairie's Edge, Santa Fe, New Mexico.

Page 115: Buffalo shield , courtesy Prairie's Edge, Santa Fe, New Mexico; painted background by Mary Beth Thielhelm.

Page 119: Rotten Belly shield and rattle, courtesy Prairie's Edge, Santa Fe, New Mexico.

Pages 122–123: Deer skin rug and Thunder Horse stick, courtesy Prairie's Edge, Santa Fe, New Mexico; Beaded tobacco pouch, collection of Harriet and Seymour Koenig.

Page 126: Painted background by Mary Beth Thielhelm.

Page 129: Deer antler handle knife, courtesy Prairie's Edge, Santa Fe, New Mexico.

Page 133: Painted deer hide pictograph, courtesy Prairie's Edge, Santa Fe, New Mexico; Sioux beaded gauntlets, courtesy Friedman Gallery, Westport, Connecticut.

Page 141: Apache dolls, collection of J. M. Eppinger.

Page 144: Zuñi bowl, collection of Harriet and Seymour Koenig.

Page 149: Sioux beaded ration card holder, c. 1885–1895, courtesy Historic North American Indian Art, New York.

Page 153: Silver squash blossom necklace and wooden bowl, courtesy The Common Ground, New York.

Page 156: Papago canteen, courtesy Historic North American Indian Art, New York.

Page 161: Apache basket, courtesy The Common Ground, New York; Navajo rug, private collection.

Page 168: Rug and Squash Kachina, collection of Harriet and Seymour Koenig.

Page 173: Hopi headdress, collection of Harriet and Seymour Koenig.

Page 176: Zuñi bracelet, courtesy Historic North American Indian Art, New York.

Page 180: Silver concho belt, courtesy The Common Ground, New York.

Page 185: Zuñi Bear fetish, courtesy Historic North American Indian Art, New York; Navajo rug, private collection.

Page 192: Navajo rug, private collection.

Page 201: Tlingit totem, c. 1910–1920, courtesy Jeffrey R. Myers Primitive Arts, New York; pottery crock and bowl, courtesy American Classics Gallery, Westport, Connecticut; painted background by Mary Beth Thielhelm.

Page 204: Spoon courtesy The Common Ground, New York; painted background by Mary Beth Thielhelm.

Page 213: Elk Dreamer Antler quirt, courtesy Prairie's Edge, Santa Fe, New Mexico; painted background by Mary Beth Thielhelm.

Pages 216–217: Painted background by Mary Beth Thielhelm.

Page 221: Haida goat horn spoon, c. 1880, courtesy Jeffrey R. Myers Primitive Arts, New York.

Page 224: Tlingit Shaman and wolf cub halibut hook, c. 1870, courtesy Jeffrey R. Myers Primitive Arts, New York.

Pages 232–233: Maricopa figure, courtesy The Common Ground, New York; painted background by Mary Beth Thielhelm.

LINE ART CREDITS

Page 1: Pecos, New Mexico, pottery design, from *Decorative Art of the Southwestern Indians* by Dorothy Smith Sides (New York: Dover Publications, 1961). Used by permission.

Page 7: Painting from Ralls County, Missouri, from *Rock Art of the American Indian* written and illustrated by Campbell Grant (New York: Thomas Y. Crowell Company, 1967). © Campbell Grant. Used by permission.

Page 14: Pecos, New Mexico, pottery design, from *Decorative Art of the Southwestern Indians*.

Page 15: Borders and symbol, from *American Indian Design & Decoration* by LeRoy H. Appleton (New York: Dover Publications, Inc., 1971). Used by permission.

Page 18: Southern Appalachian incised pottery design, from *American Indian Design & Decoration*.

Page 19: Above, shell gorget with two woodpeckers; below, shell gorget with two turkeys, from *Etowah Papers* by Warren King Moorehead (New Haven: Yale University Press, 1932).

Page 20: Mississippi pottery design, from *American Indian Design & Decoration*.

Page 21: Red painting, from Meyer Springs, Texas, from *Rock Art of the American Indian*.

Page 22: Border and pattern, Cherokee basket weave design; Seminole sun and moon, or moon and star, from *American Indian Design & Decoration*.

Page 24: See page 18.

Page 25: One element of the Creek Green Corn *(boskita)* ceremony, engraved on a conch shell found at Spiro Mounds, Oklahoma, from *America's Ancient Treasures* by Franklin and Mary Elting Folsom, illustrations © Rachel Folsom (Albuquerque: University of New Mexico Press, 1983). Used by permission.

Page 26: Border, Southern Appalachian pottery pattern, from *Authentic Indian Designs: 2500 Illustrations from Reports of the Bureau of American Ethnology*, edited by Marcia Naylor (New York: Dover Publications, 1975). Southeastern design, from *American Indian Design & Decoration*. Used by permission.

Page 27: Southern Appalachian pottery pattern, from *American Indian Design & Decoration*.

Page 28: Border, see page 20. Cherokee incised pottery pattern, from *American Indian Design & Decoration*.

Page 30: See page 18.

Page 32: Seminole rainbow beadwork pattern, from *American Indian Design & Decoration*.

Page 33: Pecked bear tracks, North Carolina, from *Rock Art of the American Indian*.

Page 35: See page 22.

Page 36: See page 20.

Page 37: Engraved shell, Tennessee, from *American Indian Design & Decoration*.

Page 38: See page 26.

Page 40: Border, see page 22. Design motif, from *American Indian Design & Decoration*.

Page 41: Design motif, from *Authentic Indian Designs*.

Page 42: See page 20.

Page 44: See page 18.

Page 45: Stone disk from Carthage, Alabama, with serpent and human hand, from *Authentic Indian Designs*.

Page 46: Border, see page 20. Pecked bird with speech symbol, eastern Missouri, from *Rock Art of the American Indian*.

Page 48: See page 32.

Page 49: Pecked drawing of thunderbird motif, Missouri, from *Rock Art of the American Indian*.

Page 50: See page 26.

Page 51: Mississippian winged serpent, from *Elements of South-*

eastern *Indian Religion* by Charles Hudson (Leiden: E. J. Brill, 1984).

Page 52: See page 18.

Page 53: Borders, from *American Indian Design & Decoration*. Engraved Adena tablet, from *Prehistory of North America* by Jesse D. Jennings (New York: McGraw-Hill, 1968).

Page 58: Iroquois woven moose hair design, from *American Indian Design & Decoration*.

Page 59: Iroquois design, from *American Indian Design & Decoration*.

Pages 62–63: Border, Menominee design and beadwork design from Menominee woven bag, from *American Indian Design & Decoration*.

Page 65: See page 58.

Pages 66–67: Border, Potawamani beadwork design; Eastern Cree beadwork on cloth, from *American Indian Design & Decoration*.

Page 68: Mohawk woven moose hair design, from *American Indian Design & Decoration*.

Pages 70–71: Border, see page 58. The Iroquois Washington Covenant Belt, from *American Indian Design & Decoration*.

Page 72: Design from Menominee woven bag, from *American Indian Design & Decoration*.

Page 73: Ojibway quillwork design on buckskin bag, from *American Indian Design & Decoration*.

Page 74: Border, see page 62. Engraved Adena tablet, from *Prehistory of North America*.

Page 75: Engraved Adena tablet, from *Prehistory of North America*.

Page 76: See page 66.

Page 78: See page 68.

Page 79: Pecked Algonquin thunderbird and other figures, Susquehanna River, Pennsylvania, from *Rock Art of the American Indian*.

Page 82: See page 72.

Page 84: Border, see page 62. Incised drawing of cranes, Wisconsin, from *Rock Art of the American Indian*.

Page 86: See page 58.

Page 88: Border, see page 66. Bird-claw ornament from Hopewell, Ohio, from *Indian Art in North America: Arts and Crafts* by Frederick J. Dockstader (Greenwich, CT: New York Graphic Society, 1960).

Page 89: Hand from Hopewell, Ohio, from *Indian Art in North America*.

Page 90: See page 68.

Page 92: See page 72.

Page 93: Engraved Adena tablet, from *Prehistory of North America*.

Page 95: See page 62.

Page 96: Border, see page 68. Maple syrup paddles, from *Pleasing the Spirit*, by Douglas C. Ewing (New York: Ghylen Press, 1982).

Page 97: Borders, from *American Indian Design & Decoration*. Warrior on horse, from *Rock Art of the American Indian*.

Page 102: Arapahoe design from painted rawhide bag, from *American Indian Design & Decoration*.

Page 103: Detail of Pawnee buffalo robe painting, from *Rock Art of the American Indian*.

Page 104: Hidatsa design from painted buffalo robe, from *American Indian Design & Decoration*.

Page 106: Border, Blackfoot design from quillwork, from *American Indian Design & Decoration*. Pecked figure, Wyoming, from *Rock Art of the American Indian*.

Page 107: Red rock painting, Meyer Springs, Texas, from *Rock Art of the American Indian*.

Page 109: Painting on shield, from *Pleasing the Spirits*.

Page 110: Border, Nez Perce design from woven bag, from *American Indian Design & Decoration*. Stylized incised figure, Rice County, Kansas, from *Rock Art of the American Indian*.

Page 111: Stylized incised figures, Rice County, Kansas, from *Rock Art of the American Indian*.

Page 113: See page 104.

Page 114: Dakota border, from *American Indian Design & Decoration*.

Page 116: Border, see page 106. Incised shield figure, Castle Gardens, Wyoming, from *Rock Art of the American Indian*.

Page 117: At left, red painted shield figure, Fergus County, Montana; at right, pecked shield figure, White Canyon, Utah, from *Rock Art of the American Indian*.

Page 118: See page 102.

Pages 120–121: Border, see page 110. Buffalo from *American Indian Art* by Norman Feder (New York: Abrams, 1971).

Page 122: See page 104.

Page 124: Border, see page 106. Incised foot from Nebraska, from *Rock Art of the American Indian*.

Page 125: Thunderbird and ceremonial figure, Medicine Rapids, Saskatchewan, from *Rock Art of the American Indian*.

Page 127: See page 114.

Page 128: See page 110.

Pages 130–131: Border, see page 114. Grouse-track, from *American Indian Design & Decoration*.

Page 132: See page 104.

Page 134: See page 102.

Page 135: Pecked footprints and abstract designs near Tulare, South Dakota, from *Rock Art of the American Indian*.

Page 136: Border, see page 106. Pecked foot from Lake Pend d'Oreille, from *Rock Art of the American Indian*.

Page 137: Borders and Mimbres pottery design, from *Decorative Art of the Southwestern Indians*.

Page 145: Hohokam pottery design, from *Rock Art of the American Indian*.

Page 146: Ancient Pueblo pottery design, from *Decorative Art of the Southwestern Indians*.

Page 147: Ancient Pueblo pottery design, from *Decorative Art of the Southwestern Indians*.

Page 148: Ancient Pueblo pottery design, from *Decorative Art of the Southwestern Indians*.

Pages 150–151: Border, ancient Pueblo pottery design, from *Decorative Art of the Southwestern Indians*. Basket and pottery designs from Pima, Arizona, from *Decorative Art of the Southwestern Indians*.

Page 152: Border, basket design from Pima, Arizona, from *Decorative Art of the Southwestern Indians*. Moki drawings of squash blossoms, from *North American Indians of Yesterday* by Frederick S. Dellenbaugh (New York: G. P. Putnam's Sons, 1900).

Page 154: Ancient Pueblo pottery design, from *Decorative Art of the Southwestern Indians*.

Page 155: Pecked design, from *Rock Art of the American Indian*.

Page 158: Border, modern Hopi pottery design; Acoma pottery design, from *Decorative Art of the Southwestern Indians*.

Page 160: Southwestern basket design, from *Decorative Art of the Southwestern Indians*.

Page 162: Pueblo pottery design from Laguna, New Mexico, from *Decorative Art of the Southwestern Indians*.

Page 163: Navajo dry painting, from *Decorative Art of the Southwestern Indians*.

Page 164: Pueblo motif from San Ildefonso, New Mexico, from *Decorative Art of the Southwestern Indians*.

Page 166: See page 146.

Page 167: Mimbres pottery design, from *American Indian Design & Decoration*.

Page 169: Pueblo motif from San Ildefonso, New Mexico, from *Decorative Art of the Southwestern Indians*.

Page 170: Border, see page 154. Mimbres pottery design, from *American Indian Design & Decoration*.

Page 171: Mimbres pottery design, from *Decorative Art of the Southwestern Indians*.

Page 172: See page 152.

Pages 174–175: Border, see page 160. Above, pecked mountain sheep; below, black painting, from *Rock Art of the American Indian*.

Page 177: Modern Navajo rug design, from *Decorative Art of the Southwestern Indians*.

Page 178: Border, see page 150. Modern Navajo rug design, from *Decorative Art of the Southwestern Indians*.

Page 182: See page 148.

Page 183: Mimbres pottery turkey design, from *America's Ancient Treasures*.

Page 184: See page 164.

Page 186: See page 162.

Page 187: Design motif, from *American Indian Design & Decoration*.

Page 188: See page 152.

Page 190: See page 158.

Page 191: Mimbres pottery design, from *Decorative Art of the Southwestern Indians*.

Page 193: Modern Hopi pottery design, from *Decorative Art of the Southwestern Indians*.

Page 194: See page 164.

Page 195: Pottery bird form, from *Decorative Art of the Southwestern Indians*.

Page 196: Border, see page 148. Design motif, from *Decorative Art of the Southwestern Indians*.

Page 197: Borders, from *American Indian Design & Decoration*. Horned animal, from *Rock Art of the American Indian*.

Page 203: Haida carved slate dish, from *American Indian Design & Decoration*.

Page 205: Red painting, from *Rock Art of the American Indian*.

Page 206: Shaman's hat border design, from *American Indian Design & Decoration*.

Page 207: Pecked Tlingit mythological bird, from *Rock Art of the American Indian*.

Page 208: Border, Tlingit basket design, from *American Indian Design & Decoration*. Red painting, from *Rock Art of the American Indian*.

Page 210: Lillooet waves or ripples basket design, from *American Indian Design & Decoration*.

Page 211: Red, white, and black painting, from *Rock Art of the American Indian*.

Page 212: Yurok basketry design, from *American Indian Design & Decoration*.

Page 214: Border, Yurok basketry design, from *American Indian Design & Decoration*. Red and white painting, from *Rock Art of the American Indian*.

Page 215: Pecked figure, from *Rock Art of the American Indian*.

Page 216: See page 210.

Pages 218–219: Border, see page 208. Elk, mountain sheep, and other game animals, Salmon River, Idaho, from *Rock Art of the American Indian*.

Page 220: See page 212.

Page 222: See page 206.

Page 223: Northwest coast bear design, from *Indian Art of the Northwest Coast* by Edward Malin and Norman Feder, illustrated by Bill Holm (Denver: Denver Art Museum, n.d.). Used by permission.

Page 225: Haida scoop net design, from *American Indian Design & Decoration*.

Page 226: See page 208.

Page 227: Pecked Tlingit mythological creature, from *Rock Art of the American Indian*.

Page 228: See page 210.

Pages 230–231: Border, see page 214. Deer and mountain sheep, Inyo County, California, from *Rock Art of the American Indian*.

Page 232: See page 212.

Pages 234–235: Border, see page 206. Northwest coast thunderbird, eagle, and hawk, from *Indian Art of the Northwest Coast*.

Pages 236–237: San Ildefonso pottery design, from *Decorative Art of the Southwestern Indians*.

We have endeavored to obtain necessary permission to reprint the works of art in this volume and to provide proper copyright acknowledgement. We welcome information on any oversight, which will be corrected in subsequent printings.

CONTRIBUTORS

Arthur D. Amiotte, who wrote the introduction and notes on the recipes for the chapter "The Great Plains," is an enrolled member of the Oglala Sioux Tribe. He is a poet, artist, writer, and consultant on Indian cultures of the Northern Plains and is Adjunct Professor of Native Studies and Art at Brandon University in Brandon, Manitoba. He was previously the chairman of the Lakota Studies Department at Standing Rock Community College in Fort Yates, North Dakota. He serves as a Senior Advisor to the Director of the National Museum of the American Indian, Smithsonian Institution, Washington, D.C., and has received many awards for his writing and his art. He lives in Custer, South Dakota.

Co-author **Beverly Cox** grew up on a ranch near Cheyenne, Wyoming, where she developed a strong interest in Native American culture. As a child, she remembers visiting the Oglala Lakota who came to Cheyenne for the annual Frontier Days, particularly Princess Blue Water, a granddaughter of Sitting Bull, who was a friend of her mother and her grandmother. Her family also made regular trips to the Indian Ceremonials in Gallup, New Mexico, a meeting place of tribes from across the nation. She now lives in Connecticut, and works as an independent food consultant, recipe developer, and food stylist. She was culinary director, food editor, and director of food styling for *Cook's Magazine*, and her articles have appeared in *Food & Wine*. This is her sixth cookbook.

Martin Jacobs, co-author and photographer, has had a strong interest in Native American culture since he studied the Eastern Woodland tribes in grade school. He is a professional photographer based in New York City. His photographs illustrate the *Foods of Vietnam*, published by Stewart, Tabori & Chang in 1989, which received the prestigious IACP/Seagrams Award for best cookbook of 1989.

Clara Sue Kidwell, who wrote "Native American Food," and the introductions to the chapters on "The Southeastern Coast and Woodlands" and "The Northeastern Coast and Woodlands," teaches in the Native American Studies program at the University of California at Berkeley and is a trustee of the National Museum of the American Indian. One of her special interests is Native American medicine, health, and diet, and she teaches a course on Native American medicine. Dr. Kidwell is a member of the Chippewa Tribe of Minnesota through her mother, and of the Choctaw tribe of Oklahoma through her father. Her Choctaw grandmother lived with her family as she was growing up, and was a significant influence on her life.

Harriet Koenig, an anthropologist with a specialty in American Indian cultures, wrote the chapter introductions and notes on the recipes for "The Southwest" and "The West." She is Lecturer in the Department of Anthropology at the University of Connecticut, Stamford Campus. She has toured Europe, Israel, and Japan for the United States International Communications Agency, speaking on current social, political, and economic aspects of Navajo and Pueblo societies. She was co-curator for the exhibition "Sky, Sand and Spirits" at the Hudson River Museum in Yonkers, New York, in 1972 and for two exhibitions at the Katonah Gallery in Katonah, New York: "Hopi Clay, Hopi Ceremony" in 1976 and "Navajo Weaving, Navajo Ways" in 1986. She has lectured on Southwestern Indian culture in public and private schools, for adult education programs, and for museums. Since 1959, her studies have been enhanced by frequent visits to reservations, particularly in the Southwest, where she has made lasting friendships with many Native Americans.

INDEX

DESIGNED BY JIM WAGEMAN

COMPOSED IN ICONE AND IN LITHOS BY
TRUFONT TYPOGRAPHERS, INC.,
HICKSVILLE, NEW YORK

PRINTED AND BOUND BY
TOPPAN PRINTING COMPANY, LTD.,
TOKYO, JAPAN